UNLOCKING
POTENTIAL

UNLOCKING POTENTIAL

*7 Coaching Skills That Transform
Individuals, Teams, and Organizations*

Michael K. Simpson

GRAND
HARBOR
PRESS

Published by Grand Harbor Press, Grand Haven, MI
www.brilliancepublishing.com

ISBN-13: 9781477824009
ISBN-10: 1477824006

Cover design by Faceout Studio, Tim Green
Interior visuals by Faceout Studio, Emily Weigel

Library of Congress Control Number: 2014932185

UNLOCKING
POTENTIAL

CONTENTS

FOREWORD

Dr. Marshall Goldsmith

Michael Simpson's *Unlocking Potential* is a skillfully written treatise about how you can be a great coach In the book, Michael coaches you on how to be a better manager-coach; as a result, you, your people, and your organization can thrive. In this book, you'll find the paradigms and key principles that are essential for you to coach effectively from and to any level of the organization.

This book is such an important work because in all my years of coaching and all my work with senior leaders, I've found that one of the most common complaints direct reports have is that their managers do a poor job of providing coaching! Validated in 360-degree feedback scores for 30 major corporations, the item "provides effective coaching when needed" consistently scores in the bottom 10 of all items when direct reports evaluate their executives.

There are a number of reasons why managers tend to do a poor job of coaching. For one thing, executives are often managing knowledge workers, that is, people who know more about their work than their boss does. How can a manager be expected to coach someone who already knows 10 times more about his or her job than the manager does?

In *Unlocking Potential*, Michael identifies seven key skills that every great coach needs to help transform people into great employees. None of these include detailed instructions on how a knowledge worker should do his or her work! Michael and I agree that people want ongoing communication with their managers concerning the "big picture"—how their work is making a difference, and suggestions about how they can improve.

Another reason managers might avoid coaching is because they are so busy with their own jobs. If you view coaching as a complex and time-consuming process, you won't do it! And because your direct reports are as busy as you are, they may not want or need coaching to be a time-consuming process. As Michael points out, they want it to help them break through from one level of performance to another. They want help becoming better.

Follow Michael's advice in this great book. He'll help you coach individuals without alienating them. He'll help you focus on how you can help people be successful in the future, rather than dwell on their past mistakes. He'll give you guidance on holding coaching conversations with individuals, conversations where you listen carefully and fully commit to helping them succeed. Individuals will grow and develop while you discover the invaluable rewards of helping them succeed. And—not to be discounted—your team and organization will thrive as a result!

Foreword by Marshall Goldsmith, author/editor of 34 books, including the bestsellers *MOJO* and *What Got You Here Won't Get You There*.

INTRODUCTION

Success as a leader is a difficult thing. As a leader, your success is directly measured by the success of those working on your team, and in fact *their* success is *your* success. Team members rely on you in order to succeed, and you rely on them. So whether you are a CEO, a government administrator, a department manager, a project leader, or any other kind of leader, you need to know how to *coach your team*.

The need for effective coaching has never been greater. Gallup research shows that a team that is highly engaged has double the chance of job performance and success. Engaged workers are more productive, profitable, loyal, and customer focused. Most importantly, the research *also* shows that an immediate manager has the most profound influence on an employee's level of engagement.[1]

That's why every leader, manager, or supervisor needs to become a great coach. In an era when people are required to do more with less, they can become disengaged. The essential work of a coach is to engage the team—but many leaders are ill-equipped to do that. Often, these leaders possess great functional skill, technical know-how, expertise, and training in business management, finance, accounting, operations, sales, marketing, engineering, law, or science.

But they don't know how to be an effective *coach*.

One of my clients is a key business leader in Shanghai, China. During one of our coaching sessions, he told me, "When I graduated from law school, I came out with the very best of academic, analytical, research, and legal tools. But what I was *not* trained in, and what I was not prepared for, was how to coach my people. The first day I had a boss, I had direct reports; I had peers I needed to work with—but I had absolutely no training on how to inspire them, help them to improve performance, or break down barriers. Everything I did in my role as a leader had to be done with and through other people. I had to achieve goals with other people. Everything depended upon what I was *never* taught to do."

Most of the executives and teams I work with say the same things.

What's fascinating is that people *want* you to coach them. Not long ago, Columbia University Business School surveyed ten thousand people on whether they would like to have a coach and why. Almost everyone said they would welcome some coaching. Thirty percent said they wanted coaching to help them with "life, purpose, vision, creativity, and integrity." Seventeen percent said they needed help with their "entrepreneurial" activities and with their "team, sales, and cross-cultural diversity" issues. Sixteen percent cited "leadership and management" needs. Eight percent wanted help with "relationships," and another 8 percent sought help with "career transitions" and "future job planning and career development." Many asked for help with behavior change, leadership effectiveness, and work–life balance.[2]

Clearly, coaching is not just about the organization or the team. Coaching is about *people*. And that may seem like an over-whelming task, one that requires more than your business training prepared you for. Of course, you can be a good coach or a bad coach. And there are no reality-show judges to watch you coach and tell you whether you're doing a good job or not. But if you follow the few vital universal principles in this book, you will likely do just fine.

Much of what we do for each other every day in the way of guidance and support is a type of coaching. But coaching is more than consulting or advising: it's a specific set of competencies, skills, and behaviors, and it takes a certain kind of good intent and character. Perhaps the best definition of coaching is "unleashing or unlocking the potential of another human being." We like the definition because it's so exciting—human potential is truly infinite and at the same time totally personal. Everyone has unique strengths and challenges.

We all have had coaches who have helped us along the way, and more than likely, they were more than just a boss or a trainer. They could speak not only to our business habits and performance but also to our personal lives and our betterment as individuals. In fact, sometimes our best coaches are cowork-ers, spouses, and friends—people without authority to speak organizationally but whom we trust to give us mentoring and advice.

In the end, coaching is about positively impacting one person's mindset, heart, and behaviors so that person is never the same again. It is about helping one person make the contribution only he or she can make in the world.

Sometimes it's helpful to define coaching in terms of what it is *not*.

- Coaching is not ordering people around because you have authority or a title.
- Coaching is not "fixing" a person.
- Coaching is not creating dependency or indulging in "open-ended therapy."

Coaching is about building a relationship of trust, tapping a person's potential, creating commitment, and executing goals. *Trust, potential, commitment,* and *execution.* In this book, you'll learn about these four foundational principles or realities of coaching and how to apply them. By aligning yourself with these principles, you will become far more effective at coaching than you are now.

The word *coach* comes from a literal coach—the wheeled kind that used to be drawn by horses and carried people from one place to another. In the 1800s, college students would seek someone to "carry" them through their examinations, someone they trusted to help them excel and keep them committed—and they informally called this person a "coach." As a coach, your task is to help people break through from one level of performance to another.

Life is made up of a series of tests, trials, and great opportunities. Some are momentary, but most take endurance. These are stages of professional development that are the determining moments of the future. We've identified seven key skills every great coach needs to use to help to transform people at the individual, team, and organizational level of performance:

1. Build trust.
2. Challenge paradigms.
3. Seek strategic clarity.
4. Execute flawlessly.

5. Give effective feedback.
6. Tap into talent.
7. Move the middle.

To paraphrase my mentor, Dr. Stephen R. Covey—coaches are neither born nor made. Great coaches choose to be great coaches.

PART ONE

FOUR PRINCIPLES
OF
COACHING

1.
TRUST

All effective coaching is based on building trust, tapping potential, creating commitment, and actually executing goals. Consider how successful a coach would be who is unreliable, fails to tap into the potential of the team, doesn't trust others, doesn't know how to get the team to commit, and presides over a team that fails to execute and achieve its most important goals. The success of all coaches comes "from the inside out." Unless coaches internalize, model, and live by these principles, they will fail!

In this section of the book, we examine each of these principles and how to apply them. If you can "coach" yourself to live by these principles, you will be well on your way to helping others as a coach.

The International Coaching Federation (ICF) has published a set of ethical standards[3] for coaches. Among other things, all professional coaches pledge to:

- Show genuine concern for the individual's welfare and future.
- Continuously demonstrate personal integrity, honesty, and sincerity.
- Keep confidences.

Everyone agrees that only a person with these traits can be trusted, and the first requirement of coaching is to be trusted.

Of course, these are all ethical traits. We can understand them, have the will to live by them, and even preach them to others. We can do all these things and still be untrustworthy. It is only when these traits are modeled and become part of our very being that we can be fully trusted.

Simply being in a position of authority does not make you a trusted coach. Your concern for the person you are coaching must be based on genuine and good intent. Your integrity must be inviolable. Your determination to keep confidences must be unshakeable.

At one point in my career, I accepted a role working as the sales and marketing vice president working along with the executives at a company that had solid growth potential.

Before I accepted the position, I observed that the executive team had changed its sales leadership and sales force every few months. The longest anyone had lasted in my position was eight months.

I soon learned why the company had a history of turnover: low trust and poor employee morale. On the surface, the CEO came off as intelligent, focused, and ambitious, but there were many broken promises and hot-tempered interactions fueled by his larger-than-life ego. The rapidly growing company was burning through funding at an alarming pace. Every member of the leadership team—particularly the sales team—felt enormous pressure to execute.

Still, I was excited about our prospects. I established a clear sales strategy, defined a clear value proposition to differentiate our technology in the marketplace and to market to key customers and channels by setting up goals and objectives, and improving our service support with core customers.

Even as our success grew, I soon learned that in executive team meetings, only one opinion in the room mattered: the CEO's. My attempts to manage my sales team were largely ignored or blocked. Tense weekly executive meetings usually dissolved into finger-pointing and micromanagement.

Shortly before I was due to finalize a contract that would bring a large commission to me and one of my associates, the CEO called both of us into his office and announced that we were fired, effective immediately.

We showed him the client commission report with the payout we had earned. The CEO sat back in his chair and grinned. "Let me remind you that you are an at-will employee. I can fire whomever I want, whenever I want."

We argued that he owed us the commission, based on the signed contract. He ordered his fellow leader who was in the room, "Have them removed from the property immediately."

My mind was reeling. I had never witnessed or experienced such immoral or unethical behavior. My associate's friend was an attorney who offered to pursue a lawsuit. I felt justified in seeking vengeance. I was angry. I had been betrayed.

Then early one morning when I was fretting in my study, my wife, acting in the role of a personal coach, came to me. "I don't think you should pursue this," she said gently, "even though I know what happened was completely wrong. I don't want the spirit of contention in this house as you conduct a year or two of depositions and relive this situation over again and again. Our positive energies need to be pointed towards our future without constantly revisiting the past."

My wife continued to coach me to change my thinking about an intensely painful and unjust situation. If it had been someone else, I might have shrugged off the advice, but because I trust my wife, I listened and was able to let go of a bad situation that was consuming me. Her coaching helped me reframe a negative situation into new opportunities. She asked me a series of very helpful questions: "What have you learned from this situation? What would be the benefit of moving forward? What would be the costs of seeking justice? Do other previous sales leaders really want to go through depositions and relive past injustices? How can you best move forward from this negative situation? What are the benefits? What would you like your future career path to look like? Where are your greatest skills, gifts, and passion going forward?" As she asked me these very powerful questions, I started creating a clear plan that would build a bridge to a better future.

Coaches ask insightful questions that help people gain greater awareness of their situation and help them reframe and creatively explore new and better ways to move forward.

I trust my wife so thoroughly that I was willing to let her counsel guide me. Of course, to earn this kind of trust, it took years and deep understanding of one another. In the workplace, coaches rarely have that kind of time and awareness, but they can still show a high level of genuine concern, good intent, and ask great provocative questions.

Your intent here matters. You have their best interests foremost in mind. You talk straight to them. You listen empathically, help them see and explore options forward, and show respect to them. These are issues of character—*your* character. If you can't show genuine concern, if you're distracted, or have other priorities on your mind—stop. Train yourself to stay in the moment with the person whom you are coaching, to keep your mind focused solely on that person's, life, leadership, career, or performance agenda. Your goal is to be on their agenda, not your agenda.

FranklinCovey has surveyed more than 54,000 people, asking them to identify the essential qualities of a great leader. Integrity is by far the number-one quality, according to the global respondents. Stephen M.R. Covey confirms what the survey found: "The ability to establish, extend, and restore trust with all key stakeholders—customers, business partners, investors, and coworkers—is the key leadership competency of the new global economy."[4] Why is trust the most important of all leadership competencies? It drives and enables success with all other competencies.

Stephen M.R. Covey helped to lead the merger between two companies, the Covey Leadership Center and Franklin Quest Company. The merger between these two firms was extremely difficult and fraught with many challenges. The challenges of distrust were vast because of merging strategy, structure, values, communications, and the alignment of two very different cultures that had been competing against each other for many years. As this company was led from a place of distrust during the merger, to a culture of high trust many years later, FranklinCovey is one of the most respected and trusted leadership development companies in the world. Much of what Stephen M.R. had experienced on both trust and distrust during the merger led to his research and writing in his world class best-selling book *The Speed of Trust*. You'll recall in a previous story that I had with a boss who operated from an approach that was the exact opposite of my experience being led by Stephen M.R. Covey. My previous leader used a very industrial and authoritative approach to leadership influence. This leader conveniently acted in expedient and short-term ways that he felt added value, but his method of influence was to influence others around him through spinning data, misinformation, politicking, fear, intimidation tactics, and the manipulation of people and data. He managed upward very well with the Board of Directors and with our executive team but had very little respect with the majority of the people across the organization. As I reflect on the vast difference between these two leadership styles, Stephen M.R. Covey had very high integrity, good intent, great capability, and consistently delivered great results. The other leader had very poor integrity and selfish intent and failed to inspire and unleash the talent and passion of his direct reports and staff. He was very smart, intelligent, and expedient, but was never able to sustain results because people across the organization did not trust him. Those who worked with Stephen M.R. Covey knew of his genuine care, empathy, integrity, and his ability to act in win–win ways and to entrust those around him. He focused on leveraging, building, and uplifting team members strengths, seeing the good in others, and showing real value and rewards for their contribution. As a result, those who worked with him felt like a trusted and loyal partner and they were fully engaged and motivated to work hard and produce extraordinary results. The famous basketball coach John Wooden was famous for saying, "I'd rather be out in front leader with a banner, than as a leader behind with a whip." Some leaders operate in business like it's the child's game, "Whack a Mole." This is where the leader pulls out a baseball bat and continues to whack people on the head by catching them doing things wrong, rather than catching them doing things right. Their motive is to beat people up, destroy their confidence, and demoralize them by treating them in unkind, discourteous, and disrespectful ways. Much of this is due to a leader's lack of emotional intelligence or his or her personal ego, or insecurity.

An executive coach working with senior members of a large automotive company learned the power of keeping confidences. He was assigned to work with a small group of very experienced, technically skilled leaders. Their technical expertise, however, was far more advanced than their skill in managing people. Their business was having tremendous success, capturing opportunities their competitors were not technically able to address. But the growth was straining their workforce, and some strain came because of the poorly developed interpersonal skills and lack of emotional intelligence among their leadership team.

One of the leaders was gruff, standoffish, and openly rude, and came very unwillingly to the coaching experience. Three weeks into the process, something was said in one of the group coaching debrief sessions that offended him. He responded very aggressively, pointing his remarks at the coach. The coach maintained integrity to his principles and did not respond in kind.

In that moment, everything changed.

Afterward, the same rude leader asked to meet with the coach personally. He said he'd been very impressed with how the coach handled the stressful situation with a high degree of emotional self-regulation, and how he now felt comfortable beginning to build a relationship. He told the story of his career and life, his successes and failures. Despite his gruff exterior, he was actually seeking help to find a better path forward. Recognizing the extremely personal nature of the disclosures, the coach made it clear that the conversation would be kept completely confidential. "I know," said the leader. "I've been watching you work with others. I've been listening to the stories you share and how you share them, and I'm confident you'll be as careful with me and my story as you have been with theirs."

Drawing close to another person requires profound trust. It should never be taken lightly and should always be handled wisely and professionally. When people allow themselves to be vulnerable, the coach must be committed to keeping personal information strictly confidential. It is the most important aspect of the coaching role. Indeed, the lifeblood of truly great coaching is absolute confidentiality.

Trust is hard to earn but easy to lose. It can take weeks and months of gentle and careful nurturing to gain trust—whereas one broken promise, one display of indifference, or manipulation with bad intent, or one failed confidence can ruin everything. That's why *trust* is the first principle of coaching. All effective coaching starts with the understanding of the great obligation to be trustworthy.

2.
POTENTIAL

All coaching is customized; by that we mean that the coaching agenda is always driven by the person *receiving* the coaching. Organizations often engage either internal or external coaches to help leaders become more successful, or in some cases to be "fixed" as a leader or manager, but even though the organization's interest is in its improvement of organizational strategies and goals, coaching is always a one-on-one, personal activity.

Like a custom tailor, a good coach finds out what the individual wants and then takes the measure of the individual. A good coach does not try to fit someone into "a ready-made suit." A good coach starts with the individual's own vision and then leads him or her to prioritize those things that are most important in achieving that vision.

Coaching is about finding and growing the potential of individuals to achieve goals important to them and to their organization. Coaching is based on the assumption that everyone can grow and that everyone has the potential to become something better, regardless of the point of departure. It is true that some will struggle more than others, but everyone can achieve new and better things that they might have initially felt beyond their reach.

Understanding the individual's priorities, potential, and goals takes time and requires listening, observing, reflecting, and customizing your approach so that the person's uniqueness can be leveraged.

We do that by first understanding the individual's story, context, and point of view. Then we can help reframe that point of view if necessary so the person's own potential can be fulfilled.

All people have stories: where they've been in life, where they are now, and where they want to be someday—in a week, a year, or five years from now. These stories tell you much of what you need to know about their potential. The stories reveal what's important to them, what they hope and fear, what keeps them going. These stories can also be focused on what are their unmet needs, barriers, or opportunities that they see among their key relationships, customers, marketplace, or within the business and team. Surveys, 360-degree assessments, colleague interviews, skills and aptitude tests, and work records are helpful to uncover people's stories, but there's no substitute for hearing about their dreams, hopes, desires, disappointments, failures, and fears from their own mouth.

A good coach must set personal stories aside and invest fully into listening to, engaging with, and feeling the power and the potential of the individual's story. As the relationship matures, the coach can reflect the person's story back from a more objective, detached perspective, unobscured by layers of pain, disappointment, frustration, and misguided efforts.

One of my coaching clients opens up about everything. "We close the door and talk about what is going on, both positive and negative, not just in my professional life. I feel safe. We talk about where I need help, tensions with my boss, frustrations with our company culture, where people are allowed to act in ways that are totally inconsistent with our company values. I talk about my own shortcomings—that I'm impatient and even rude with people I think of as stupid."

At the simplest level, coaching is a process of paying full attention to a person. When we pay attention to people, they light up. Even as a child, we have an instinctive response to personal attention, respect, and positive feedback. That need for human response does not end when we become adults. When people are truly listened to, when they can *see* that others are listening, they begin to open up, engage more, and expose potential suppressed by years of self-defensiveness, self-betrayal, or self-denial.

Thus, a great coach is an active listener, affirming the miracle of being human, addressing the potential, rather than the limits, of what each person can do. Coaches reflect, facilitate, and amplify. They partner with individuals to generate positive and uplifting strategies for future action. Coaches know that adhering to fundamental coaching principles and practices—"coaching presence"— that is, *being with the individual in the moment*—matters more than technique and style. The coach offers a fine balance between inquiry and advocacy.

A great coach gathers information by listening with the heart for feelings, listening with the ears for content, listening with the eyes for visual cues to that which is not verbalized. Really effective coaches pick up even the smallest of cues. When an effective coach is at work, a spirit-to-spirit element of communication comes into play.

Point of View

As I've said, the best coaches learn to listen and observe beyond the story line itself. They pay attention to revelations of behavior that come from more than just words. Becoming sensitive to the physical and emotional context, as well as the verbal context, makes better coaches.

You must learn to rely on all of your senses during coaching sessions. Sometimes during a coaching conversation, an individual may seem to be sharing openly, yet without divulging important information. In these instances, a good coach must rely on senses other than sound—by learning to "look beyond the words" for information and insights from nonverbal cues.

Watch for the following behaviors:

- *Physical Behaviors.* These include yawning, looking down, avoiding eye contact, gesturing with the hands and arms, folding arms, and so on.
- *Verbal Behaviors.* Patterns of language, verbal tone, avoidance of key issues, repeated references, or common topics or themes continuing to arise in the conversation are all verbal behaviors. An individual who keeps returning to a particular person, event, or feeling is signaling that the theme may be a dominant feature of that individual's story or perspective. Or, the avoidance to talk about certain events, people, or feelings may be a signal as well.
- *Emotional Behaviors.* Elements of a story may provoke emotional reactions that are particularly strong or surprising. These are emotional clues that, if observed, go beyond simply placing a single experience in an overall life story. They can tell an observant coach how much power or influence the moment of that experience has had on the overall story.

Try looking through a set of binoculars at some sporting event: immediately you will grasp the concept of "point of view." With binoculars, you can sit in the cheapest of the cheap seats, way up at the top of a stadium, and still watch the action as if you were sitting in the best seats right at ground level. It isn't that the game itself changes; rather, your perspective or point of view is modified by the lenses through which you are watching it.

In coaching, the individual's perspective can be helpful or hurtful. Some have excessively critical or negative points of view, where others' perspectives are too optimistic. Some of the people you coach will struggle because of overabundant passion and self-confidence; they see their own potential as unlimited. Others will be timid and discount their own potential too much.

Sometimes their point of view is evident in the elements of the story itself; sometimes it's not. You may need to carefully probe for greater understanding. You do this by listening with *empathy*. Empathy is not listening to someone in order to advise, counsel, reply, refute, fix, judge, solve, change, agree, disagree, or to figure the person out. Empathy is the ability to accurately reflect what the person is feeling, experiencing, and saying. Great coaches create a safe environment where people simply feel understood.

Challenge Paradigms

Deeply held views that color every aspect of a person's thinking are called "paradigms." A person's paradigms may or may not correspond to reality. A man whose paradigm is that women are over-emotional might have a hard time working with women. A woman whose paradigm is that of a man is controlling and dominant might have a hard time working with a man. An individual who is motivated only by money might lose interest in other aspects of personal growth, balance, and fulfillment.

Our paradigms can help or hurt us. Our paradigms can limit us in achieving our potential, thus becoming self-fulfilling prophecies. People afraid of failure interpret setbacks as confirmation that they are failures. They may also be risk averse, hindering, and judging of those who seek to innovate or who make mistakes or have failures. In turn, they become less likely to try for success—so their faulty paradigm becomes "true."

A coach can help people shift people's paradigms by challenging them. For someone who has struggled in the past, a coach can help them look back on hard times and reframe those experiences through a positive lens. The coach can help the individual ask, "How did that difficult experience benefit me? What was the growth or learning opportunity in it? If I could change this situation, what would my ideal situation look like in the future?"

When Caroline Casey turned 17, she tried to apply for a driver's license. The problem was, Caroline was blind. Never having defined her blindness as a disability, she was taken aback when officials laughed at her for requesting a license. Her paradigm was that she was not at all disabled. Her parents had never told her she was disabled, so from her point of view she could do anything anyone else could do. It was a revelation to her to learn otherwise.

Prevented from choosing one path, she chose another. She went to India and rode an elephant—which did not require a license—across the country. She then circumnavigated the globe, using 80 different forms of transport. Today she helps businesses change their point of view to better accommodate disabled people.

As a coach, your task is to help individuals change paradigms that are holding them back from achieving their potential.

The late computer-science professor Randy Pausch turned his imminent death into a lesson on living. Informed by doctors at age 46 that he had only a few months of good health left before he would die of pancreatic cancer, Randy decided to make use of every last minute of his life. He got himself invited to speak to the U.S. Congress on the need for more cancer research; he delivered an upbeat lecture at Carnegie Mellon University on "Really Achieving Your Childhood Dreams"; and he wrote *The Last Lecture*,[5] a positive, forward-looking book translated into 46 languages and featured on *The New York Times* best-seller list for 85 weeks.

Most consider setbacks as omens of failure. This is a faulty paradigm. If you can help people see their perceived deficiencies in the framework of overall proficiency, they can overcome that paradigm. Randy Pausch's example demonstrates that people can shift perspectives and turn their greatest challenges into opportunities.

When a coach helps a person challenge their paradigms, they can more readily take responsibility for their life or situation. When they learn to align their paradigms to reality, many of the barriers to realizing their potential begin to fall.

Psychiatrist David Burns identifies some common patterns of thinking that are based on unrealistic paradigms. People jump to conclusions with all-or-nothing, absolutist thinking ("He always (or never) responds that way to my requests") or discount positive experiences ("She only helped me on that project because she wanted all the credit").[6] The coach's job is to challenge these assumptions, test values and intent, and help the individuals towards a more realistic view of themselves and their situation.

My colleague, Fatima Doman, coached a client who struggled with stress-related health challenges, including bouts of anxiety that led her doctor to suggest that she seek stress-management coaching. A devoted wife and mother, she also headed a nonprofit organization in South America and was regarded as a high achiever and a role model for others. But she was plagued by fears and doubts that caused intense distress, and she often found herself incapacitated for hours at a time.

In coaching sessions, she recounted memories of her childhood. She was raised in a loving home but was surrounded by illness and excessive worry. She watched a family member struggle through a long, terminal illness from his birth until his death in his twenties. These experiences clouded her response to stress in her life as an adult.

After coaching and practicing positive, affirming self-talk, she began focusing on the evidence that her work at her nonprofit organization was important. The more light she shed on her fears, the more they scattered, providing space to release and eliminate each negative thought as it appeared. Although she had felt fear, she could now recognize courage and optimistically move on with her life despite some of her negative history and difficult life experiences.

We challenge paradigms by imagining the world as viewed through different lenses. It takes imagination to envision something different and better than the negative stories people tell themselves or those inaccurate stories we may tell or believe ourselves. Coaches can help people begin to see the fruits of their own potential instead of the ashes of their limitations. Coaches can help fuel, support, and fire that imagination.

3.
COMMITMENT

It's easy to motivate people in the short term. A persuasive pep talk, an immediate reward, an urgent threat—all these external motivations can move people to action. But they don't last. Once the urgency is gone, the motive goes with it. The only kind of commitment that lasts is internal commitment.

That's why creating lasting commitment is another key principle of effective coaching.

But how does a coach create commitment in the individual?

Of course, you can't require commitment from others, but you can create the conditions where people commit to goals they themselves want to achieve.

The principal skill for creating commitment is to ask powerful coaching questions.

In her book *Change Your Questions, Change Your Life: 10 Powerful Tools for Life and Work,*[7] respected executive coach Marilee Adams says that life's toughest issues are not solved by having all the answers, but by asking the right questions. Coaches who continue to ask powerful and provocative questions help individuals develop a sense of internal purpose and commitment for the long run. In a sense, a coach's main job is to ask the right questions at the right time.

Of course, coaches must always remember that the opportunity to coach comes with an obligation to honor people's right to be in charge of their own story and, ultimately, the outcomes of the coaching experience. Questions should not be manipulative.

Along with asking questions, a coach should remember to talk less and listen more. Most of your talking should consist of asking powerful questions with active listening. I use the word *powerful* because the questions actually provoke commitment and assign the heavy lifting and real work to be performed by the individual. As a coach, if I tell people what to do and how to do it, it becomes my responsibility, not theirs, whether it works or not. The individual then can come back and say, "Okay, coach, I did what you told me to do and how you told me to do it, and it didn't work—and now what do you want me to do?" Individuals don't take ownership of commitments that doesn't belong to them.

Of course, your questions will often naturally follow the pattern of the conversation. In most conversations, casual or formal, once a person begins to share her story, aspirations, or struggles, the sharing can prompt appropriate, intuitive follow up questions. But coaches have an obligation beyond simply being very capable conversationalists. They must focus on helping individuals, teams, and organizations achieve strategies, prioritize goals, shift perspectives, and keep commitments. This is best done by questioning. During my Columbia University Coaching Certification Program, our director Dr. Terry Maltbia taught our session a structured framework to engage others in a natural coaching conversation.

The powerful questions a coach asks may fall into three areas:

1. Engaging with purpose (Opening)
2. Advancing to commitment
3. Obtaining commitment (Closing)

First: Engaging with purpose. Start by asking insightful questions that get the individual thinking about purpose, whether it's the purpose of the whole coaching engagement, or the purpose of today's meeting, including the desired benefits of it, that may include:

- What specific needs, issues, or opportunities bring you to coaching?
- What are the most important strategies, goals, or outcomes that you need to accomplish personally or professionally?
- What do you want to accomplish as a result of our coaching relationship?
- What legacy do you want to leave in your life/your family/your career?
- What do you see as your "best self" five years from now?
- What contribution can you make in your current role at work?
- What do you need to achieve this year?
- Can you make that goal more specific?
- How will you know when you've achieved that goal? How will you measure success?
- What will be different as a result of the time we spend together today?

Once the individual has envisioned a goal, the challenge is to figure out how to achieve it. The individual isn't likely to commit if the goal seems too lofty, vague, or difficult, whether the goal is to turn a profit, improve a relationship, better engage a team, or to lose weight.

Second: Advancing to commitment. Your questions should help the individual move towards both logical and emotional commitment. Your task here is to help the individual anticipate and take down barriers to achievement.

- What are you currently doing that is working towards your goal?
- What are the obstacles? How have you addressed similar situations in the past?
- If you had unlimited resources—time, money, people, information, technology—and knew you could not fail, what would you try?
- What resources (including time, money, people, information, technology) do you have that you can call on?
- What are the benefits of going after these anticipated goals and key outcomes?
- What would be the costs or negative outcomes of not doing these things?
- What is the single most important thing to do now to advance towards your goal?
- If you went to your respected person or expert with your problem, what would this person suggest to you?
- If you saw someone else in your situation, what would you recommend?
- On a scale of 1 to 10 (with 10 being highest), how motivated and likely are you to make your goal happen by that time frame you have committed to? How might you alter the plan to move it closer to a 10?[8]

Third: Obtaining commitment. Obtaining commitment involves summarizing, narrowing the focus, and selecting options and confirming next steps. These questions allow coaches to "circle the conversational wagons" and bring summary and clarity to all of the shared information and feelings.

Closing the conversation requires that individuals have a clear and memorable summary of what they are committed to do next in pursuit of their personal goals and aspirations for change. This is what we call "confirming" the conversation.

- What are the two or three most important things for you to focus on before our next coaching session?
- Based on what we have discussed, what seems most important for you to focus on now?
- We have talked about a lot of important information today. If you were to put headlines on the key areas you want to focus on, what would they be?
- What will you do in the next 24 hours (or week or month) to move forward towards your goal?
- On a scale of 1 to 10, how motivated are you to take care of this commitment?
- What will it take to turn that rating of a 6 into a 9?
- Can you think of anything that might stop you from doing it? How will you overcome that barrier?
- Moving from vision and big picture, what actions would you like to focus on over the next 30, 60, or 90 days?
- What do you need to do to help fulfill this commitment going forward?
- How will you measure your success? What milestones or key successes will be important for you to achieve with your game plan?
- What do you see as the best way of holding you accountable?

Creating commitment is the essential closing stage in the coaching process. Commitment arises from inside out; any attempt to impose commitment means the individual will never truly take ownership of it.

That's why powerful questions are such important tools for the coach to gain buy-in from the performer. A skillful questioner can help individuals speak their own language, set their own goals, promote their own reasons, and offer their own solutions when they encounter problems. A coach must never forget that individuals create their own stories—we can't do it for them. Great coaches set the right high-trust environment and safe conditions for people to transform themselves by doing the necessary heavy thinking and lifting. Dr. Stephen R. Covey says, "Change—real change—comes from the inside-out not from the outside-in. It doesn't come from hacking at the leaves of attitude and behavior, by telling or advising, by fixing or teaching . . . It comes from striking at the root—the fabric of our thought, the fundamental, essential paradigms, which give definition to our character and create the lens through which we see the world."[9]

4.
EXECUTION

Once an individual has made a commitment, the coach's next task is to help that person execute and be held accountable. The principle here is obvious: unless there is execution and accountability, the coaching engagement becomes just a fruitless series of ongoing conversations. All successful coaching conversations need to link directly to actually meeting key performance indicators, measures, and objectives. How does an effective coach help individuals execute?

Coaching is working to discover the precise nature of an individual's desired destination. What is the overall scope of the engagement? The challenge for a coach is to help the individual find this desired destination without the coach imposing his or her own personal paradigm, vision, values, or passion.

A coach's duty is not to define the journey or push people along a path where they may not want to go. Rather, coaches help individuals keep their hands on the steering wheel so they can both drive and arrive. Foundational to helping people grow is to disengage them from the negative and the limiting, and to engage them in the positive and expanding.

Inherent in the ideas of growth and achievement is the optimistic expectation that things *can* change, and *will* change for the better.

Executing worthwhile goals usually requires continuous, often repeated efforts of accountability. To meet a sales goal, to get a product out the door, to help a student towards a degree, to get stronger, or to lose weight—the individual has to keep working at typical goals like these. Often, the individual lacks staying power and the commitment to the right behaviors or habits to sustain lasting change. Taking the first step is often hard enough—contemplating the thousandth step can be wearying.

However, a coach knows that repeated effort can also become easier over time. Repeated actions become habits. Moreover, the best coaches can actually help individuals get into a "flow" state that can be exhilarating for them.

Get into the "Flow"

What is the flow state? Psychologist Mihaly Csikszentmihalyi defines "flow" as a feeling of great inner clarity and energy that comes from total absorption in a task.[10] We often hear athletes talk about the "high" of being "in the flow." When flow is powerful and purposeful, people have optimal energy, full engagement, even bliss; they describe feeling like they are floating along a river.

Just as a river moves towards a determined point, people in a flow state move towards a defined destination inherent in their mission. The flow state sustains the insights and impacts through the coaching experience. Flow empowers individuals to move beyond their coach as they pursue their dreams. Great coaches try to achieve and sustain flow with their individuals.

Recall "Flow" Experiences

One way to help individuals get into the "flow" is to ask them:

- Think of a time when you were in a high performing "flow" state.
- When are you are your best?
- How did it feel?
- What kept you going?
- How do you think you could get into the flow state of high performance now?

"Flowing" doesn't happen by accident. It requires practice and persistence to create flow. For one thing, according to Mr. Csikszentmihalyi, "It is not enough to know how to do it; one must do it consistently, in the same way athletes and musicians must keep practicing what they know in theory."[11] Getting into the flow is quite different from experiencing practice and repeated effort as drudgery. The flow state leads to high levels of self-mastery, self-confidence, and fulfillment at the same time.

Discover "Flow" Behaviors

Another way to get individuals into the flow is to help them find some new activity to enjoy, something they are good at, that leads towards the goal. Some people never experience flow because they remain stuck in old paradigms, old habits, and fruitless practices that are emotionally draining or boring. Coaches can help individuals discover new and better behaviors that generate flow.

Business mogul Sir Richard Branson has never been afraid to challenge himself. His list of achievements and the fact that his face is plastered on advertisements everywhere belie the fact that he is by nature rather shy. His dyslexia resulted in poor academic performance as a child, and he never finished formal schooling due to his learning disorder, but that never stopped him from pursuing his personal and professional aspirations. In time he discovered he was a great visionary and good at making connections with people. His companies have had their ups and downs, but in 1992 he sold the Virgin label for $1 billion to fund Virgin Atlantic Airways. Today the Virgin Group encompasses more than 200 companies in 30 countries—and keeps Branson very busy. Despite his many setbacks in business, he is known for his imagination, hard work, and passion to push the boundaries of innovative success.

How does he keep it all going? He is in flow with people and ideas. He exudes a high degree of appreciation, optimism, and trust in others, reframing negatives into positives, and inspiring those around him to join the flow of innovation and new ideas. He's always ready to step into the river and be flooded with energy and new ideas. Even when he's in a meeting, he may lie down on a couch to ease brainstorming with his guests. If he hears a great idea and doesn't have a notebook handy, he'll jot it down on the back of his hand. What matters to him is the free flow of ideas, and he does whatever it takes to keep that tap flowing.

While in the flow state of high performance, people have more energy and self-awareness, and they find themselves completely immersed in what they are doing. How can you help the people you are coaching find those new behaviors that will get them into the "flow"? Ask these questions:

- What are the most important unmet needs, challenges, difficulties, or opportunities that society is asking you to solve?
- What is the highest and best contribution you can make to humanity?

- What legacy do you want to leave? What difference do you want to make?
- What have you always loved doing? What are you really good at?
- What are you most passionate about?
- What professional or career-related opportunities are you most excited to pursue?
- What unique talents or abilities can you bring to the goal? What do you do best? What have others told you you're good at? Where have you received acknowledgment?
- What feels like play to you—meaning that when you engage in that activity, time seems to fly by, and you feel happier and lifted up?

One of the great musicians in history was Glenn Gould, an award-winning Canadian pianist. As a child he loved music but couldn't stand practicing the piano. His teachers were frustrated. But Glenn found his own way to master the instrument: he loved intensively studying his music books and scores and was able to commit them to memory, visualizing himself playing and interpreting the music in his own way even without touching the piano.

After many hours of such study, Glenn would sit down at the piano and perform what he visualized in his mind. His unique way of getting into the flow led him to become a world-famous, one-of-a-kind concert artist. The example of Glenn Gould shows that there is more than one way to get into flow—in fact, there are probably as many ways as there are people or opportunities to do so.

Persist in Practicing "Flow"

A habit is simply a groove or a pathway in the brain. Repeated activity of any kind eventually creates such a groove, and you are able to do the activity without thinking about it, almost subconsciously or effortlessly. The execution of goals often requires routine, habitual work.

Consider American swimmer Dara Torres, who participated in five Olympics, taking home 12 medals, including four gold medals. At the age of 41, her time in the event that got her to the Beijing Olympics in 2008—the 100-meter freestyle—was 2.47 seconds faster than her Olympic time in 1988 at age 21. Most would assume that a woman of 41 could not participate, let alone excel, at the level required for the Olympics.

Torres found her own ways to get into the flow and then made it habitual. Every day she went through a series of what one sportswriter called "weird invented exercises. She churned out push-ups with her feet suspended in leather straps . . . She plunged off a tilted wood block with a resistance cord attached to her waist, as if she was diving into an imaginary pool. Almost nothing she did using the equipment at the fitness center matched the instructions for how to use the equipment."[12]

Torres achieved her goals by inventing her own way into the flow and staying there habitually. Flow becomes habitual, and habits in turn sustain flow.

Ask the individual you are coaching:

- How much time and effort will you need to commit to pursue this opportunity?
- What one thing could you do each day that would get you closer to the goal?
- What habits do you need to form?
- What habits do you need to change or eliminate?

So here we are, hopefully with a better understanding of the principles that underlie the practice of coaching. These principles grow out of a fundamental desire to help and an ethical framework that guides that desire. These principles infuse all types of coaching—personal, team, and organizational. Although the principles remain the same, the application varies based on the audience, and in the next few chapters, I am going to show how these principles can be applied in actual coaching situations.

PART TWO

SEVEN COACHING SKILLS

Coaching is far more than showing up and counseling, giving pep talks, consulting, advising, or telling people what to do. It's a definite skill set. With practice and the right intent, I believe any leader or manager can get really good at coaching. The good news is, anyone can master it. Whether you're coaching executives of large corporations or five-year-old soccer players, you need the following seven skills.

1. Build trust. This is the foundational competency and skill of all great coaching—without it, individuals will suspect you, question your agenda, slow you down, and possibly reject you as a coach. That's why it's the first skill of coaching.
2. Challenge paradigms. A paradigm is the way we think. An individual who believes they can't improve is not coachable—until that paradigm changes, you'll go nowhere. Your individual's paradigms might become barriers to

achievement, and as a coach, your task is to challenge them firmly and gently.

3. Seek strategic clarity. With the coach's help, the individual should choose personal goals and be completely clear about them with measurable endpoints. Without strategic clarity, coaching becomes aimless and endless.

4. Execute flawlessly. Execution might be the toughest challenge of all—the coach can help individuals actually to set, prioritize, and achieve their goals and help to hold them accountable.

5. Give effective feedback. All coaches give feedback. Some of it is effective. By following the suggestions in this book, you are guaranteed to give feedback that helps create awareness, focus on actions, and achieve the results that people want with whom you're coaching.

6. Tap into talent. Most people underestimate their own talents. As Dr. Stephen R. Covey would often say, "most people have far more talent than they ever use." As a coach you need to know how to help people tap into the unique and vast reserve of talents they already have.

7. Move the middle. Coaches are usually focused on helping high performers get even better. It is essential to reward and promote top talent. However, the biggest opportunity for performance improvement in any organization is to help to "move the middle," among those performers who are good, but not yet great. We'll show you how to take advantage of that opportunity.

In life, as in work, one of our key leadership responsibilities is to help people gain vision and strategic clarity in their jobs, careers, and in their business.

Never forget your role as a leader is to help people through uncertainty, darkness, and the fog, so they get to their ultimate destination and achieve success.

On July 4, 1952, Florence Chadwick, who had previously swum the English Channel with success, now attempted the 21-mile swim from the U.S. southern California mainland to Catalina Island.

The water was freezing at 48 degrees. The fog was thick, and visibility offered little to no sight at all. Finally, one-half mile from completion of her destination, she became discouraged and quit. The next day reporters surrounded her and asked why she had quit. Was it the cold water, the difficult currents, or fatigue due to the distance? She responded, "I was licked [defeated] by the fog." She then recalled a similar lack of clarity due to the fog while swimming the English Channel, when the fog was equally engulfing. She was exhausted. As she reached out for her father's hand in the nearby boat, he pointed to the shore. She raised her head out of the water long enough to see the land ahead. With this new vision and clarity, she pressed on in the fog and became the first woman to conquer the English Channel.

Similarly to the way that Florence Chadwick's father pointed to the shore from the boat, leaders and managers must help coach their people and teams by "clearing the path" and helping them see opportunities and success by gaining a clear vision and strategic direction in the midst of the fog among many urgent, distractions.

It's not the hard work that tires people out—it's the fog!

5.
BUILD TRUST

Great coaches place a premium on establishing, developing, extending, or restoring trust with the people whom they are coaching.

Often trust is overlooked as a hidden variable. And yet we can all cite situations where low trust is evident. All we have to do is glance at the media headlines concerning global economic markets, corporate scandals, banking and government improprieties, and abuses in the world of politics, entertainment, or athletics. We can find low trust in educational, religious, and charitable organizations. Only 39 percent of employees trust their senior leaders, according to the Watson Wyatt Work USA study, and only 45 percent of employees have confidence in their management teams.[13] Almost half of employees reported observing misconduct that, if revealed, would cause their firm to "significantly lose public trust," according to a KPMG 2000 Global Organizational Integrity Survey.[14]

The role of a coach is twofold: (1) to help the individuals themselves become more trustworthy and (2) to establish a trusting relationship with individuals and key stakeholders. In your first role, you earn trust by being a model of character and competence. In your second role, you know you're being effective when your individuals and key stakeholders consistently attract loyal people to themselves—people whom they position, empower, and reward—successors who are prepared to lead even better than they themselves do. You know when there is trust in the organization when leaders actively get others promoted, build a pipeline of talent, and try to create leaders to replace themselves.

Trustworthiness might sound a bit traditional or old-fashioned—like something you'd talk about at a Boy Scout meeting—but it is absolutely current and necessary. Why? Because trust translates into *individual credibility*. Each individual leader, manager, or coach has a personal brand of trust or distrust. Credibility comes from the Latin root *credere*, which means "to believe." Anyone you expect to successfully coach others must first believe in *you*.

In his best-selling book *The Speed of Trust*,[15] Stephen M.R. Covey describes two sources of trustworthiness: character and competence. Character is who you are—your personal maturity, integrity, and commitment to principles. An immature, unprincipled person cannot be trusted regardless of his or her skills. Your competence is what you do—your talents, skills, and capabilities. Even a person of high character cannot be trusted if they lack the skills to do the job in a high quality way. Both character and competence are essential to have trust and credibility.

We have said that trust is the first principle of coaching, and it bears repeating. As a coach you must model both character and competence yourself first, before you can expect it of others. Your interactions with the individual must be beyond reproach. Your own honesty and integrity are your stock-in-trade; you can't afford to raise questions in the person's mind about your agenda. A coach is, by definition, in a position of trust.

Your competence is a matter of mastering the skills taught in this book. What you are ultimately doing is creating *leaders,* trustworthy people who can challenge their own paradigms, strategize for themselves, execute flawlessly, and tap into the talents and resources available to them. So all effective coaching starts with your character and ability to build a trusting relationship with leaders you are creating and developing around you.

Your task is also to help your individuals become more trustworthy themselves. They are going to be leaders; therefore, they must be trustworthy people by modeling the espoused values of the team and organization.

Diagnose Character

What is the individual's intent—that is, their motives and agenda? No one is willing to follow a leader whose motives are suspect. Motives must be open, transparent, and mutually beneficial.

Think about it: When you suspect someone has a hidden agenda, are you not cautious and reticent to be fully engaged?

How do you help an individual become more trustworthy? This is accomplished not through lectures so much as through asking the right questions:

- Whom do you trust and why?
- Whom do you mistrust and why?
- Who trusts you as a coach or leader?
- What are you doing to earn the trust of others?
- What kind of relationship do you want with your boss [your coworkers, your spouse, your kids, your market, your customers, your employees]?
- What's your motive?
- If you act on that motive, what kind of results do you think you'll get? In the short term? In the long term?

Let individuals define for themselves the outcomes of suspect motives.

A coach who helps abusive husbands overcome their behaviors relies heavily on questions like these. Instead of lecturing to abusive men on the law, morality, and relationship psychology, he asks them questions like: "What kind of relationship do you really want with your wife? What kind of behavior on your part will create that relationship? What's your motive for hitting her? What do you think the outcome will be if you act on that motive? What do you see happening down the road if you continue to behave this way? Do you take this same abusive behavior at home into the workplace?" By constantly asking these questions again and again, this coach helps husbands become more self-aware—of their hopes, their wishes, their motives, self-betrayal, and the inevitable consequences of their actions. Often, this approach brings a real awareness and change in behavior.

Diagnose Competence

And that brings us to another element of trustworthiness: *results*—track record, outcomes, the ability to get the right things done. If leaders don't accomplish what they are expected to, their trustworthiness decreases. The converse is equally true: When leaders achieve the promised results, they establish a reputation as producers—and trust increases.

To diagnose the competence of the people you are coaching, ask questions:

- What is your track record?
- What would others say about your ability to do the job and consistently get results?
- What do you think about your ability to do the job and consistently get results?
- Where do you need to improve your abilities?
- What can your team realistically do?
- Where does your team need to improve?

The purpose of these questions is to bring to the surface strengths to capitalize on and weaknesses to work on. The idea is to help the individual identify areas where trust might be enhanced.

One example of a high-trust coaching engagement that I had was with a world-class U.S. National Football League (NFL) football organization and its owner—we'll call him Mr. Jones for the sake of privacy.

Mr. Jones was a highly respected and successful businessman and a well-known philanthropist in his metropolitan community and within the state. He had established a strong brand, emphasizing family values, and community involvement as the owner of the team.

He hired me as an executive coach for the leadership team within his organization. During this coaching engagement, I observed his great leadership and vision, and his generosity to the community and the organization. He extended high-performance expectations and high trust to the leadership and players on his team and to the coaching staff.

Although I cannot share the confidential details regarding our engagement, I can summarize some overall coaching themes and impressions from my experience. The leadership team has become a great model of the leader-as-coach that exemplifies trust, empowerment, and credibility at all organizational levels. This was first modeled and exhibited by the owner creating a culture of strategic clarity, clear goals and objectives, high expectations for success, and ongoing accountability, as well as establishing a strong culture of family values and loyalty to his team members.

Mr. Jones purchased the team to help bring the community together and to put forward a great product that would inspire trust and success with all stakeholders. His charitable foundation is a great model for offering generosity to at-risk youth as well as donating generously to education, art, and culture. Mr. Jones also personally donated more than $150 million to various other charities. When he acquired the team, he was already a trusted leader. Everyone knew that his intent was positive, and his integrity and track record were unquestionable.

After the NFL franchise was rocked by scandal and a succession of several different coaches, Mr. Jones knew he had to change the way business had been done. While breaking in a new, untested quarterback, Mr. Jones gave his coaching staff and management team the freedom to make choices. Trusting and empowering the leaders around him to hire the right talent paid off and that influenced the most successful winning seasons in the franchise's history.

Mr. Jones saw the value in coaching and that it would significantly help his leaders to further align their decisions with his organizational values, and help take their personal and professional performance to an even higher level of success. Thus, he offered to coach leaders in order to help set the right values and tone at the top, which in turn, began to make its way throughout the organization.

Our monthly executive coaching meetings were with the head football coach and his general manager which focused on both personal and professional issues, challenges, and opportunities for success. The team also took measures to clearly empower their assistant coaches, players, and staff with better decision making skills, planning, prioritization, and execution. They wanted them to have a greater sense of purpose in their work and to seek opportunities for personal and career growth. The team also valued the importance of work–life balance and wanted to promote a sense of family among their leaders and staff. Specific opportunities were created for his leaders and their families in order to become involved in giving back to the community.

It was clear to me that Mr. Jones' own expression of modeling trust, and his sincere desire to empower others, began to permeate the entire organization in a very short period of time. Mr. Jones's desire to further entrust and empower his leadership team set the right tone at all levels to begin trusting and modeling the right behaviors to further build commitment, motivation, and engagement across the organization. A coach, whether an external coach like me, or an internal coach like Mr. Jones, must first and foremost establish the right culture of values, performance, and trust. As the leader seeks to model the right values and behaviors, the overall organization will begin to feel free to empower others, and thus a culture of trust will be born organization wide.

6.
CHALLENGE PARADIGMS

As I've said, our paradigm can limit us in achieving our potential. Recall that a paradigm is a point of view or a way of thinking. So many paradigms are obstacles to improvement: a view of oneself as inadequate or untalented or victimized. As a coach, your task is to help individuals shift paradigms that limit their progress. You can do this by questioning those inaccurate or limiting paradigms.

Throughout this book, I've used powerful questions to demonstrate how a coach can help create an opportunity for increased self-awareness and transformational change. The great master teacher Socrates asked pupils questions that challenged the accuracy and completeness of their thinking. He stated, "The unexamined life is not worth living." In a way, that moved his students towards have humility and inquiry to learning and discovery. Let's look at five categories of questions he used to challenge paradigms, thinking, and assumptions:

1. Explore Assumptions

Ask questions that help individuals think about and test the presuppositions and unquestioned beliefs or values on which they are basing their leadership or their work styles. Your job is to shake the deep bedrock of their thinking and help them go to even deeper levels of reasoning. Here are examples of such questions:

- You seem to be assuming that such and such is the case. Why is this the case?
- What underlying values or perceptions seem to be driving these actions?
- How did you choose those assumptions?
- Please explain why or how you're thinking this . . .
- How can you verify or disprove that assumption?
- If you were to share the facts or the data on this situation, what would they be?
- What could we assume instead?

2. Probe Rationale

When an individual gives a rationale for opinions and assumptions, dig into that reasoning rather than assume it as a given fact. People often use weak logic, reasoning, or support for their arguments. The following questions help them examine the evidence behind their beliefs:

- Why is this happening?
- How do you know this is the case?
- Can you explain to me or give a rationale of what is going on?
- Can you give me an example of that?
- What are the impacts of this situation?
- What data, facts, or evidence would give you reason to believe that?

3. Question Viewpoints and Perspectives

Most arguments are given from a particular position. You should feel free to question the positions. Show that there may be other, equally valid, or alternative viewpoints.

- What is another way of looking at this? Does this seem reasonable?
- What are your alternatives?
- That's an interesting theory. Is there another approach you should consider?
- What are the strengths of your argument? What are the weaknesses?
- Who benefits from this?
- What would someone with the opposite viewpoint say?
- What is the difference between this scenario and that scenario?

4. Examine Implications and Consequences

Often people have not thought through all the possible outcomes of a proposition. Encourage a complete exploration of all the possibilities by asking the following:

- Do the intended consequences or outcomes make sense? What are the desirable outcomes and benefits? Is there a clear and logical business case for action?
- If you achieve the desired outcome, then what would happen?
- What are the positive and/or negative consequences of that assumption?
- What are the risks or the costs/benefits?
- What is the overall economic value of doing that?
- What are the risks or the costs of not doing that?
- What might possibly happen that you haven't thought about yet?

5. Question the Question

You can help individuals examine their paradigms by turning the question in on itself. In a sense, you are making the individual do the heavy lifting.

- Why would I ask you that question? What was the point?
- Why do you think you are asking yourself this question?
- Is this question important? Why or why not?
- What assumptions are behind the question?

Coaches must be alert to the need of individuals to challenge the validity of their old paradigms. Often, people are afraid to test and question their assumptions—a coach can help take the fear out of the process by making it a natural and positive step. Coaches can help everyone adopt the attitude of positive inquiry, effectively challenging old paradigms, and innovatively embracing change. Thomas Kuhn put it this way, "all significant breakthroughs [in performance results] come from break-withs in old ways of seeing."

When I was coaching the leaders of a billion-dollar chemical firm, one of the top executives was uneasy about his job, but he didn't exactly know why. It was a great position, and he was making a real difference.

One day I conducted a workshop, and this leader attended. In the workshop, I introduced what I call the "Whole Person Paradigm"—that a person has physical, emotional, mental, and spiritual needs. We are not satisfied as a "whole person" unless all of those needs are met.

When it came time for our coaching session, he told me that his paradigm had shifted. He had not been thinking of himself as a whole person. Here is what he said:

I have been running the business for eight years with double-digit growth and have been executing very well. Ninety percent of our teams are hitting their targets, and we have had one of our best growth years in the history of this company. I have built a very solid leadership team.

But am I motivated to stay with this company for the long term? Are my whole-person needs being satisfied?

Currently I'm making very good money, and if I leave this company, I will forfeit a lot of money; a lot of commissions and bonuses will be left on the table. So my current physical needs for money are very well satisfied. The heart or social emotional need is also fully satisfied: My boss, who is the CEO, is a wonderful man with high integrity, and he treats me very well. The family and the business have been loyal to me. The company has taken very good care of me, and I am deeply indebted and loyal to them.

But as I look at things with a whole-person mindset, I have become aware that I want to take my professional career to the next level. I really believe I need to be more challenged intellectually. To be more fully engaged in my career, my mind and my intellect need more global and strategic challenge and development.

As his coach, my task was to help him challenge his own paradigms. The paradigm shift he experienced helped him move on to a more challenging, but more intellectually rewarding, position with another company. This was a very difficult move for him, but through coaching, he was able to transform his career and his life to a higher state of meaning, purpose, and contribution.

7.
SEEK STRATEGIC CLARITY

A key coaching skill is to help individuals find their destination on their own—without forcing on them the coach's own vision, values, or passions. No coach has the right to force change, to impel momentum, or to prescribe or demand a particular destination. But both the coach and individual need a destination, and fundamental to that destination is a self-chosen personal mission that is ignited by what Dr. Stephen R. Covey calls "the burning yes inside."

The coach's task is to help individuals come up with a concrete mission statement and a strategy for carrying it out. Helping people find their mission—the life purpose they are burning to say yes to—is essential to defining the new direction they wish to take. A mission not only gives purpose to life but also can unleash the power to re-focus, repurpose, and re-energize that life of meaning and passion.

My colleague, Fatima Doman, coached a client who gave his life to his job. He was a loyal, intelligent, and effective senior-level employee who loved his work. But she felt uneasy when he made the comment to her one day that the company was his life. This man also had a son, two daughters, and a wife who waited for him at home while he worked whatever demanding hours his projects required. He has been able to remain married and to have an acceptable, if not close, relationship with his daughters. But his son has turned to drugs and has been in and out of jail. When visiting his son in jail, his son said, "Dad, I'm not sure I'd be sitting here if you had been home when I needed you."

In his book *The Heart Aroused: Poetry and the Preservation of the Soul of Corporate America*, poet and lecturer David Whyte tells of a woman he met in one of his corporate workshops. The participants had been exploring why humans sacrifice their "personal vision" and their "sacred desires" to profit a company. She told him, "Ten years ago . . . I turned my face for a moment, and it became my life."[16]

Instead of grasping at things that are momentarily attractive, we must invest our time and attention to clearly define a vision—a dream we cherish deeply and one to which we are willing to give great effort and sacrifice. We must turn our faces towards that vision even in the face of immediate and pressing items on a to-do list or with the pressure to keep up with society's definition of material success.

In everyday terms, if you're not happy in your personal life, it impacts your work output and how you interact with your coworkers. And the converse is also true: If you're not happy in your work life, it affects how you act when you walk through the door at home or meet with your friends. If you're not achieving "what really matters most to you," it affects you in every way—mentally, physically, spiritually, and emotionally.

A manager at a university, coached by my colleague Fatima Doman, was promoted to a top administrative post. Far from celebrating her success, she found her promotion to be so stressful that she became nearly incapacitated by her fear of failure. She spent countless overtime hours at work, stopped exercising in an effort to squeeze out more time in the day, started living on fast food from the vending machine, and eventually gained 30 pounds. She couldn't sleep soundly. Her anxieties spilled over into her personal life. She found it impossible not to think about work while at home.

During coaching, she spent time clarifying her mission and purpose, both personal and professional. When she became clear on what was truly important to her, she was able to repurpose and better focus on balancing all four dimensions of life: physical, mental, spiritual, and social/emotional. She now begins each day at work by listening to inspiring music, places fruit and healthful snacks within eyesight on her desk, takes at least one stress break during the day for a 15-minute walk, attends an exercise class twice a week, and has moved her chair so that she can see the trees from her office window. After doing these few things, she performed so well in her new job that she was promoted again—and this time she knew how to handle the stress.

Clarifying your strategic mission in life can help you achieve your potential and decrease stress. You know what to say yes to and when to say no. Coaches can help by introducing the individual to the notion of a personal mission statement, a written document with the following attributes.

A mission statement accomplishes the following purposes:

- Clarifies what is most important to the individual
- Provides focus and clarity
- Helps the individual design their own life instead of having it designed by external forces
- Guides day-to-day decisions about how to spend time and energy
- Gives a greater sense of meaning and purpose

Ultimately, a personal mission statement forms the foundation of the "burning yes inside." It helps the individual to measure life's success as well as organizational success. When people achieve things connected with their personal mission and vision, it feels wonderful to them.

My Story

In my mid-20s, I was immersed in a fast-moving, high-level career. The economy was booming, and I was surfing the corporate leadership wave. My clientele included many Fortune 500 companies as well as government agencies. As a management consultant, I influenced key corporate leaders while working side by side with many great coaches who were top performers in the field of organizational behavior and leadership development.

I knew how to help individuals uncover basic values and principles in order to craft their own personal mission statements. Those statements helped them define their vision and find their voice in their life and work. I taught them to "begin with the end in mind" and helped leaders and managers clearly define where they wanted to end up in their personal and professional lives. I helped individuals establish their vision and goals to drive their missions and strategic pathways.

I was satisfied with what I was doing, yet not satisfied with where I was going. I had a compelling vision of where I ultimately wanted to be professionally. I was teaching scientists with PhDs at Dow Chemical, Westinghouse, and Los Alamos National Laboratory, as well as experienced senior executives within various global corporations. I explored many options to take my life to the next level. I was unsure whether I should attend graduate school, gain international career experience, get married, or start my own business.

Here I was, a well-paid management consultant influencing the destiny of leaders in multinational corporations, but I lacked the strategic clarity to make decisions about my own life. With no clear vision for my future career, I became more and more frustrated and confused. Nothing seemed quite right. It was ironic that I had been teaching strategic clarity and focus to managers and leaders in my professional work each and every week, yet my personal future seemed so unclear. Why was I having such a difficult time charting my own course?

I began to do a lot of self-analysis and reflection.

Finally, after weeks of pondering my future, and while on a business trip to work with an executive team at Packard Electric, I woke up in the middle of the night, filled with the confidence that comes from hours of careful personal reflection. I jumped out of bed and began mapping out specific steps and a timetable for my future, based on my personal vision, mission, and goals. I was becoming my own executive coach.

I also sought out two coaches for guidance and direction, individuals with whom I had worked closely at my job. I had consulted with both of them on several engagements and had tremendous trust and respect for their life experiences and confidence in their guidance with my career. They helped me weigh the cost-benefits of staying or leaving, to gain much desired and needed international experience. They helped me weigh my options: a full time graduate program, outside consulting experience, or leading and managing a business.

My road map was strangely counterintuitive but became perfectly clear in part because of great coaching. It took courage to leave a well-paying job, where I worked for one of the best leaders in my field, and a large consulting firm that was more like family than coworkers. But I knew it was the right thing to do. Within two months I had sold my home, left my job, accepted a yearlong teaching post at South China University of Technology, spearheaded a management-development program for Nike in Guangzhou, China, and commenced my graduate studies in Organizational Behavior at Columbia University in New York City.

My road map made no sense in light of short-term economic benefit and my eight-year investment with a leadership-development firm that I loved. But the short-term sacrifice was right for me. In pursuit of that clear and compelling vision, I started working in a foreign country on a salary less than one-tenth of my former earnings, depleting my savings, and incurred significant debt to pursue an advanced degree at a first-tier Ivy League school. But as I diligently and rigorously followed my road map, I found myself enjoying the most astounding personal, business, academic, and cultural experiences of my entire life.

My coaches helped me develop a vision of the future with real strategic clarity, as well as a very detailed tactical plan that charted my actions and commitments to execute on that strategy. Given that the formula is so simple, it is unfortunate that more people don't find their way to living the life they love. Perhaps they succumb to the sentiment captured in this often-used statement: "In the absence of clearly defined goals, we become strangely loyal to performing daily trivia until ultimately we become enslaved by it."

> *Vision without action is merely a dream. Action without vision just passes time. Vision with action can change the world.*
> —Joel A. Barker

Short-Term Noise

Much of life can be driven by urgent short-term noise but relatively meaningless demands. By contrast, a successful career requires a clear vision, careful planning, analysis, and strategy formulation all along the way. The same is true of any effort you lead—whether it's strategic goals, a project, a team, a division, a family, or a whole organization. The coach's job is to help individuals and teams get totally clear on their vision, mission, and contribution. These personal coaching questions are helpful:

- What kind of life and what kind of career would you like to have?
- How will you measure the success of your life and career?
- What would be a successful life or contribution by your definition? What aspects of your contribution do you want to keep in balance?
- What are your most important relationships? What are you doing to keep them close, intimate, happy, and functional?
- What would compel you to get out of bed every morning, passionate to get going with your day?

- What important and meaningful things would you want these people to say about you at your funeral: A spouse, a partner, or a family member? A colleague at work? A friend?
- Why does your team exist? What purpose does it serve? What does team success look like?
- Why does your job exist? Who and what purpose do you serve? Are you sure it is the right purpose? How will you know whether you've achieved it?

The leader with a clear mission sometimes wins the game before it even starts. The will to succeed is important, but the will to prepare is even more important.
—Duke University Head Basketball Coach
Mike Krzyzewski

But a great mission is generally useless without a great strategy for achieving it. As Peter Drucker states, "All grand strategies eventually boil down to work."

To fulfill an organizational vision and mission, the strategy defines the path and the plans in how to leverage its core capabilities and resources to best satisfy its market, customer, and organizational needs. Strategy is also about how you will differentiate your value with your products, services, or technology in the marketplace. It defines a company's uniqueness and competitive advantage and consists of how to leverage your operational plans, budgets, and core resources to compete and win. And, of course, strategy defines what drives the money-making model to drive increased cash, profit, margin, growth, and additional resources.

To fulfill an individual mission, the strategy is usually simpler, consisting of personal values, goals, objectives, plans, and resources.

In general at the team and organizational level, there are two types of strategies: the competitive strategy that defines why, what, where, and with whom you will compete with your products and services; and the operational strategy that defines how you will prioritize and leverage your core operational capabilities, strengths, unique know-how, intellectual property, processes, partnerships, distribution, people, and alliances. In helping leaders develop strategy, coaches should ask the following strategic questions:

- Who are your key customers? What are their needs? How can you best add value to satisfy their needs better than your competitors?
- Where will you compete? What is your distinctive competitive advantage?
- What products or services will you provide or not provide?
- How can you best leverage your relationships among partners, customers, suppliers, and distributors?
- How can your resources best be deployed across multiple business units, geographies, and channels to support your core competitive work?
- How will you differentiate yourself operationally from your competitors?
- What capabilities should you invest in? What will you not invest in?

Once you have helped define your competitive strategy, then it's time to tell a clear, compelling, and engaging story by creating your strategic narrative with your leadership team.

The following diagram shows the elements of how to draft a strategic narrative. This framework can be used by any coach to help leaders, managers, and teams ask the right questions to help clarify their strategic direction so they can focus on the right work and execute it flawlessly. The diagram is accompanied by a series of powerful coaching questions that lead to drafting and communicating your strategic narrative.

STRATEGIC NARRATIVE

What are the competitive arena and industry forces most impacting changes to your organization?

STRATEGIC CONTEXT

Who are your key customers? What are their needs? What unique value do you provide to those you serve?

JOB TO BE DONE

What are the two to three world class capabilities that you need to leverage to best satisfy your customers?

CORE CAPABILITY

DIVISION/ BUSINESS-UNIT PURPOSE

MONEY-MAKING MODEL

How will you make money, maximize your economic payback, generate even more resources?

What are the few (four or six) key mid- to longer-term strategic moves that will help you achieve your strategic purpose over the next two to five years?

STRATEGIC BETS

SNS

STRATEGIC NARRATIVE STATEMENT

Summarize steps 1–5 into a one-page focused and compelling statement to engage your division/team over the next two to five years.

Answer these strategic questions based on your division/ business unit that you directly influence.

DRIVE STRATEGIC DIRECTION AND FOCUS

First, start by defining the "strategic context," the important industry forces and issues that need to be taken into account before you define your strategy. To define the strategic context, ask this question: What are the external forces that are changing your business environment?

Second, define your "job to be done," that is, the unique value you bring to the marketplace, the customers, and the purpose your business serves: Who are your customers (internal and external)? What do your customers hire you to do for them? How well are you doing that job?

Third, define your business unit's money-making model. How much cash do you need? What profit margin do you need to get? What is the velocity you need (speed of productivity of inventory, production, or services)? What revenue growth do you need? How can you maintain profitable and sustainable growth?

Fourth, define your core capabilities. What do you do better than anyone else? What are the one or two core capabilities you need to obtain or improve to do your job better for the customer?

Fifth, define your few "strategic bets": What competitive moves can you make that could dramatically improve your business results over the next two to five years? How will your key strategic bets help you achieve the right milestones and targets to help achieve your five to ten year vision?

Here is an example of a strategic narrative tool that offers powerful strategic coaching questions to help drive your division, business unit, and team to clarity and simplicity, so leaders and teams can clearly articulate and communicate their most important strategic priorities and objectives.

STRATEGIC NARRATIVE SUMMARY

Condense the information into a brief written summary.

 STRATEGIC CONTEXT

The key industry forces that influence our part of the SN are:

1.

2.

3.

4.

 ORGANIZATIONAL PURPOSE

1. We will create value for those we serve by:

2. We will make money/generate resources by:

3. We can leverage our capabilities better than anyone because:

 STRATEGIC BETS

The key bets we are making to win over the next 2–5 years are:

1.

2.

3.

4.

 STRATEGIC NARRATIVE DRAFT

Write a compelling one page strategic narrative to fully engage our division/team/group:

DRIVE GOAL ALIGNMENT, CLARITY, AND ACCOUNTABILITY

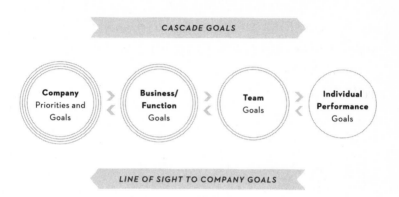

HIGH-PERFORMING ORGANIZATIONS CREATE "LINE OF SIGHT"

Once the coach has helped create the competitive strategy, it's time to set and align the right goals for making the strategy work. Without clear, measurable, time-bound goals, the strategy turns into an unused binder gathering dust on a shelf somewhere—because no one is really accountable for executing anything concrete.

A great coach helps make sure the strategy is translated into actionable goals from the top of the organization all the way down to every business unit, function, team, and even to the individual level of production. This is called creating "line of sight." Every goal at every level should be clearly connected and aligned back to the overall company vision and strategy.

Nothing reinvigorates team members like a timely reminder of a powerful and compelling goal. My colleague Bill Bennett often says, "it is not hard work that causes a person or a team to become tired; it's the fog or the lack of clarity." People need clarity about what is expected, defined targets, how to accomplish the goals, and when they need to be achieved; and that means creating concrete, realistic, and measurable goals.

In my experience, few people and organizations have clear, realistic, and measurable goals. Instead, goals usually come in the form of a fuzzy, vague slogan such as:

- "The customer is always number one."
- "Safety comes first."
- "Be better, faster, and cheaper."
- "Quality is job one."
- "Hit your numbers."

Vague slogans like these make it impossible for a team to really know what to achieve or what to do. By contrast, a concrete goal can be clearly, objectively measured and written in the following format:

"From X to Y by When."

This means: "We are now at X (current state baseline), and we want to be at Y (future state finish line) by a predetermined future date of completion (timeline)."

DEFINE WILDLY IMPORTANT GOALS (WIG)

"X"	**"Y"**	**"BY WHEN"**
The starting value for the WIG	The ending value for the WIG	The date by which the WIG must be achieved

X TO Y BY WHEN

Here are a few examples of concrete goals and objectives using the X to Y format:

- Increase profit with new product sales from $150 million to $225 million this year.
- Pay down 50 percent of our $1 million in corporate debt this fiscal year.
- Reduce customer quality concerns logged by 30 percent by Q2.
- Increase billing closure rates from 10 days to 2 days by Q4.
- Increase operational production from 82 percent to 91 percent by Q2.
- Decrease ship-to-request from 48 hours to 12 hours by Q4.
- Reduce project quotation time from 14 days to 48 hours by year end.
- Achieve 100 percent of project launch readiness as measured by green on 5Ps by Q4.
- Reduce response time from 48 hours to 8 hours with 90 percent of customers by Q3.

- Achieve 95 percent of production uptime (people and equipment) by year end.
- Achieve greater than 90 percent ratings on customer scorecard by Q4.

A great goal must be clear, specific, achievable, and measurable. General statements such as "decrease debt" would be far less actionable. "Decrease debt by 50 percent" is measurable but still weak because it gives no completion date. A more correct goal statement would be, "decrease debt by 50 percent by fiscal year end." As the late Peter Drucker said, "What gets measured gets managed, and what gets managed gets done."

With goals, less is more. In our professional and personal lives, we can always find an abundance of good things to pursue. But if everything is important, then nothing is important. When it comes to goal setting, less is more. Ten "priority" goals will dilute a team's focus quickly. A torrent of good ideas can turn into a weak trickle as energy is siphoned off to feed an overabundance of "key" goals. Helping people narrow down and select a few—maybe one to three at most—strategic goals is an important duty of a coach.

I will define these strategic priorities and objectives as "Wildly Important Goals" (WIGs). WIGs are termed the vital few most important goals that must be achieved this year to fulfill the strategy, or nothing else you achieve really matters. The idea of the WIG helps people distinguish between a lot of secondary or day-to-day goals and the critical goals that must be achieved.

Notice the difference between Presidents Eisenhower and Kennedy in the way they presented the challenge to the American people to explore space. Eisenhower said, "The U.S. needs to lead the world in space exploration." By contrast, Kennedy said: "We shall send to the moon, 240,000 miles away from the control station in Houston, a giant rocket more than 300 feet tall, the length of [a] football field, made of new metal alloys, some of which have not yet been invented, capable of standing heat and stresses several times more than have ever been experienced, fitted together with a precision better than the finest watch, carrying all the equipment needed for propulsion, guidance, control, communications, food and survival, on an untried mission, to an unknown celestial body, and then return it safely to earth, reentering the atmosphere at speeds of over 25,000 miles per hour, causing heat about half of that of the temperature of the sun . . . and do all this, and do it right, and do it first before the decade is out."[17]

Kennedy's very specific vision and goal, with its time frame, galvanized a nation to participate in that inspiring challenge. People sold their homes and moved to Florida and Texas in order to have a chance at being part of the exciting vision put forward for the future space industry. The grand goal was translated into sub-goals and projects. Everyday work in the aerospace industry was connected to a larger vision and a compelling purpose. With his precise challenge, President Kennedy provided the strategic *why* to motivate the commitment of a nation.

Coaches can help people gain tremendous clarity by posing these questions:

- What is the one goal (the WIG) that you must achieve or the strategy fails?
- What is the organization's or team's highest priority?
- What is the activity or objective without which nothing else is worth doing?
- Given the various key priorities, what can you say no to?

Certainly, many goals matter, but they pale in comparison to the most strategically or wildly important goals, and the coach must help everyone see that.

The following are a series of coaching questions that will help any leader or manager engage in a successful goal-setting process.

1. What is your role in relation to the company's vision and strategy?
2. Does your team have a sense of its most critical business gaps or business opportunities to be achieved within the next one to three years?
3. Do these gaps or opportunities directly connect with the organization's desired future vision, mission, and strategy?
4. What are the two or three most important goals that your business unit or team must achieve if you're going to fulfill your vision, mission, and strategy?
5. What are the benefits or value of achieving these goals?
6. What are the costs if you do not achieve these goals?
7. Does a clear line of sight exist between your key goals and the goals one level up?
8. Does a clear line of sight exist between your key goals and the goals one level down?
9. Does every team member know the goals, the business case, and the importance of achieving them?
10. Is every team member committed and aligned to achieve the goals?
11. Do your key goals have a valid, reliable measure that demonstrates success, and can the goal be easily tracked and measured each month?
12. Are your goals and measures truly achievable/winnable?
13. Are each of your goals written in a format, from "X to Y by when"?
14. Do we have all the right team members and resources assigned to accomplish the goals?

Coaching can help individuals define the vital few most important strategic goals in the midst of the constant noise and unimportant aspects of everyday life. Differentiating between the mass urgency of the day job priorities versus the most strategically important goals and objectives is the role of any successful leader, manager, and team.

8.
EXECUTE FLAWLESSLY

It is one thing to come up with grand strategies and wildly important goals; it's quite another to actually get them done. The more a leader is in love with his or her strategy, the more they will underestimate what it will take to actually achieve it. Once the strategy is in place, it must be enacted. One of the world's greatest thinkers on strategy, Harvard Business School's Michael Porter, famously states "It is better to have Grade B strategy, with Grade A execution, than the other way around."[18]

The leader or manager as coach has a key responsibility to help teams and individuals close what is widely recognized as the execution gap. If individuals want to excel, they must clarify first strategic purpose *and* then execute flawlessly. Without execution, the vision is just a hope, a wish, or a dream, and the best strategy will fail or be short lived at best. The inability to execute strategies and goals remains one of the main reasons why leaders, managers, and teams lose credibility and trust.

Everyone knows this. Yet the execution gap remains the biggest challenge in most organizations.

A global survey on the topics of strategy and goal execution, called the Execution Quotient (xQ) Survey, has gathered data from more than 500,000 leaders and teams across 18 global industries and 20 languages. The xQ survey results show the common challenges with strategy and goal execution. The data validates four key root causes for breakdowns with flawless execution. These challenges don't vary much across industry or culture:

1. Goal clarity. Eighty-five percent of respondents don't know the goals of the organization they work for; 44 percent of the people say they know, but when asked to identify the goals, only 15 percent can actually do it.

2. Leveraged behaviors. Eighty-five percent of the respondents don't know what to do to achieve the organization's goals. They often don't know the strategic reasons for doing the work they are doing.

3. Compelling scoreboards. Eighty-seven percent of the respondents don't know whether their company is winning or losing in relation to its most important goals. They simply don't know the score. Or if they do, they are almost always looking at historical "lag measures"—results that appear only after it is too late to do anything about them.

4. Weekly accountability. Seventy-nine percent of the respondents are not held accountable for lack of progress made towards critically important goals. Only 21 percent meet with their bosses even as often as monthly to assess achievement of their most important goals. Usually, accountability is top-down, punitive, or intimidating; or it is soft, permissive, and infrequent at best.

As a result, according to research by Michael Mankins and Richard Steel published in the *Harvard Business Review*, "Companies on average deliver only 63 percent of the financial performance their strategies promise." Generally the problem is not with strategy; the problem is with execution.

Why do individuals and teams fail so often to achieve their most important goals, even with a good strategy in place? In my experience, it's most often because they are struggling with a "whirlwind" of the day-to-day demands—lesser goals, urgent problems, and administrative issues. The strategic goals get lost in mental space cluttered with e-mails, phone calls, superfluous meetings, unnecessary reports, people's "urgent" requests, and daily routine operations. These minutiae deflect everyone from the real goals, keeping them busy, but not productive.

When day-to-day urgency comes head on with strategic priorities, urgency rather than importance usually wins. Why is this? The urgent stuff is immediate, proximate, and pressing, whereas strategic goals are usually long range, not urgent, and require new thinking and new behaviors. Think of it this way: Would individuals in your organization be busy even if they did not have a clear strategy or goals? The answer is yes—and this is a worrisome answer.

I was coaching a senior leader and his team from a large manufacturing company. He told me, "It's very easy for our staff to get seduced and caught up into what I call 'management by attention deficit disorder—MADD.' Every urgent demand and every project become all important. Urgent work becomes very shiny and attractive and we chase after it and seek to fix it immediately. It's so easy to spend all of our time running around all day jumping from one fire to another. At the end of the week we realize we have been busy, we're tired and completely exhausted, but haven't accomplished any of our most strategically important things. We've been seduced by the tyranny of the many urgent, yet less important things."

Most people can find enough urgent, administrative things to do in the day-to-day busyness of the office without ever focusing on the important goals that would best develop, unleash, and maximize their potential and output. People go to work each day and get all kinds of things done. But are they focused on getting the right things done? An individual may be working extremely hard but failing to do the most important things; under pressure, they may simply lose track of what is most significant. Many mistake activity and effort for strategic accomplishment.

So where does a coach fit in this losing scenario?

The coach helps an individual become aware of the whirlwind. Progress on goals will be very slow, temporary, or undisciplined if this conflict is not addressed early. Coaches must help individuals see the conflict between short-term, whirlwind ("urgent") activities that make up the day at work, and long-term (actually important) goals that fulfill the vision and strategy.

Often people aren't aware of the whirlwind, and so a good coach helps an individual distinguish between strategic goals and the merely urgent tasks. The coach should ask, "How does the whirlwind show up for you? If you get seduced into simply focusing on and completing the short-term urgent tasks, what will happen to your more important goals and objectives over time? What specific things compete for your time, energy, and resources? When 'urgent' and 'important' forces clash together, which one usually wins?"

Jim Collins, author of *Good to Great*, notes that what most individuals lack is discipline: "The discipline to demand results, the discipline to hold ourselves to sustained outcomes, the discipline to understand what are the inputs to produce the outputs, the discipline to build for the long term and not to succumb to expedient short term opportunity, the discipline to hold growth back to only what we can do better than anyone else in the world, the discipline to only put people in positions who are the right people for those positions—even if we feel pressure to do otherwise—the discipline to change behaviors and habits from the top all the way down to the front line. These are some of the key disciplines of greatness."[19]

The coach plays a key role in instilling those disciplines. The coach must train individuals in four disciplines of execution:

1. Focus on the "Wildly Important Goal."
2. Act on the lead measures.
3. Keep a compelling scoreboard.
4. Create a cadence of accountability.

Focus on the "Wildly Important Goal" (WIG)

What is the most important goal that I can focus on to achieve success this year? Great coaches help people realize that they will always have more good ideas than they will have time, money, and capacity to execute; therefore, they should limit their goals to no more than one to three at a time. These are the "Wildly Important Goals," or WIGs, that ask the question: what is the most important goal that must be achieved this year or nothing else matters very much? Each WIG needs to be crafted with a clear format: "From X to Y by When" so that the individual has clear direction on what needs to be accomplished by what time. Then, there is no chance of the goal becoming vague or being overshadowed by the whirlwind.

Act on the Lead Measures

What are the leveraged behaviors or proactive actions I can do this week to drive the goal towards success? As previously discussed, great coaches help individuals realize that simply focusing only on the lag measures (the final result) is futile. A sales leader might spend all week on the phone coaxing their salespeople to meet their sales goals, but it won't help very much.

Instead, the coach needs to help individuals identify the lead measures, those actions that they can control and that lead to achieving the goal. The individual must identify the real work that drives the goal each and every week. Lead measures are daily or weekly actions that are *predictive* of achieving the goal. Lead measures are *easier to influence* than lag measures but are *harder to measure*. Everyone should partner in defining, tracking, and reporting progress on lead measures daily or weekly.

Suppose the goal is to increase new sales revenue this year from $2 million to $4 million by year end. Below is a sample list of sales lead measures that are predictive, influence-able, and measureable (PIM).

- Propose two contracts to newly qualified buyers weekly.
- Make 50 outbound calls to new qualified prospects (80% get an e-marketing brochure) per week.
- Make 40 follow-up calls to targeted buyers (moving from sales pitch to close) per week.
- Obtain two new qualified referrals from existing clients weekly.

The sales leader's task is to enable the players on the team to execute these tasks proactively, and not focus solely on the sales goal. That goal will take care of itself if these lead measures have been correctly defined and showcase what the individuals and team members can actually influence. For example, instead of focusing on an annual or quarterly new sales revenue goal (lag measure), coaches must help leaders focus on, say, the number of face-to-face sales meetings conducted with a presentation to key decision makers weekly (lead measure). Lead measures are granular, influence-able, down-in-the-dirt measures and are vital to success.

Keep a Compelling Scoreboard

How do we know if everyone is engaged and winning at a game? Everyone knows by the power of a scoreboard. With scoreboards, everyone knows what everyone else is doing. People play a game differently when they're keeping score—they take it seriously. Great coaches help individuals and teams institute a regular, visible, and engaging "players" scoreboard. The potential outcome motivates the players to engage in the game. Keeping score always makes a game more interesting and engaging. Motivation increases when a player knows what the score is, who is winning or losing, and by how much. Even children become instant entrepreneurs when they are trying to sell more cookies than their friends can sell. People push themselves harder physically and intellectually when they know they will "win points."

A scoreboard must be clear—you need to be able to see what you need to know instantly: where you currently are and where you want to be at a future date. Such a scoreboard is easy to understand and is really motivating to the team. If the scoreboard is designed for a team, remember that a football player won't know the score if he's tracking only his goals. Every player must know the total score based on the entire team's performance in order to know the true position. The lead and lag measures must both be visible so that every member of the team knows whether they are winning or losing.

The following sample scoreboard allows any leader or individual team member to visibly see the Wildly Important Goal, the Lead Measures that connect the real work and behaviors that drive the goal. This visible scoreboard motivates and engages team members in a winnable game and helps them focus on how they can impact the right performance measures that drive success weekly.

CREATE A COMPELLING SCOREBOARD

1. Display your WIG as shown in the format below:

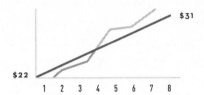

WIG (LAG MEASURE)

Increase revenue
from corporate events

(from $22 to $31 million by
December 31)

2. Design the Lead Measures that are: predictive, influence-able, and measurable.

ASSOCIATE	1	2	3	4	5	6	7	AVG
KIM	1	1	2	2	4	x	x	2
BOB	2	2	3	2	x	x	3	2.4
KAREN	1	3	2	x	x	2	2	2
TOTAL	4	6	7	4	4	2	5	2.1

LEAD MEASURE

Complete two quality
site visits per associate
per week

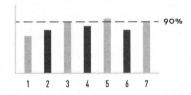

LEAD MEASURE

Upsell our premium
bar package to 90% of
all events

3. Visibly draft a "team/players" scoreboard. Display the WIGs and measures.

SCOREBOARD EXAMPLE

Create a Cadence of Accountability

Why is it so critical to hold people accountable? Without accountability, there is no commitment. An individual must account for progress not just annually, quarterly, or monthly, but weekly. Coaches can help a team so that the goal-accountability meetings are set at the same time each week. In these meetings, team members discuss personal commitments and failures in an open, candid environment while seeking to celebrate based on achieving small weekly successes. This progress report is an opportunity for learning, not judging. It helps people know if they are actually contributing towards the goal. As people help each other "clear the path" by addressing obstacles, they build support, create more positive energy, and help everyone stay on track.

According to a Harris Interactive Survey commissioned by FranklinCovey, only one in four workers meet even *monthly* with a manager to account for progress towards a goal. The survey also found that only 10 percent of respondents agreed with the statement "Team members hold each other accountable for results."[20] Many times accountability is seen as punitive, top-down, or fear based. But it doesn't have to be that way. A weekly WIG review meeting can create a rhythm and a ritual of accountability in which immediate celebration and course correction can take place.

Some things to watch out for in your weekly accountability meetings:

- Focus only on the WIG, commitments that move the lead measures, and influencing the scoreboard.
- Avoid the whirlwind, administrative issues, philosophical debates, and office politics.
- Maintain peer-to-peer communication rather than manager-dominated discussions. This meeting is not about the leader. Team members commit, report, and support each other

while holding each other accountable. Reporting is done in quick bullet points, not in long, verbose statements.

- Keep meetings to no longer than a half hour—the same time, same place, each week. The focus is on important commitments, not the urgent.
- Share weekly actions and commitments and remove roadblocks. If a team member is struggling, the team comes together to "clear the path" for that person.

A recent study by the Conference Board, a global nonprofit organization that disseminates information about business management practices, asked CEOs and leadership teams worldwide what their top ten issues were. Surprisingly, profit growth was last. Improving productivity and customer loyalty was in the bottom five. But the top two were (1) excellence in execution, and (2) consistent execution of strategy by top management.[21] It makes sense to coach people in excellent and precise execution of strategy.

Flawless execution has been called the holy grail of organizational success. Why is something that is so basic to the success of organizations—executing strategy at a team or organizational level—so rare and so difficult? How can a coach help change the mental environment and culture so that execution comes naturally?

Such a change isn't accomplished at the stroke of a pen. Flawless execution requires a change in mindset, behaviors, and skill set. Over the years, while facilitating leadership work sessions all around the world, I have asked thousands of leaders and teams to describe their common barriers to execution. Here are the top five issues they cite:

1. Too many goals at the top.
2. Unclear or shifting work priorities.

3. Most important goals are only vaguely defined.
4. Conflicting goals across peer groups.
5. Constantly changing roles and confusion over work responsibilities.

These issues from leaders, managers, and employees demonstrate a clear need for improved clarity, focus, and action. But in addressing these issues, people are going to resist change. That's why the paradigm shift of the four disciplines of execution is so essential, and your ability to coach individuals in those disciplines is the key to your success.

Holding people accountable to execute results and doing this in the right way is absolutely critical for leaders. The key is to seek to develop an empowered culture that is self-directed, motivated, and engaged with the right values and behaviors over time. Kurt Lewin, an early pioneer in the study of group dynamics and organizational behavior, identified both the "hard" and the "soft" sides of change. The "hard" side includes those cultural aspects which are visible, logical, rational, measurable variables of change, like profit and costs. The "soft" side involves people and cultural issues—that deal with emotions, values, cultural or historical contexts, style, communications, and divergent reasoning.[22] Although these "soft" side variables are less visible than those representing the hard side, they can drive or impede change. The best way to help leaders improve their organization's culture is to value and treat everyone and all issues, soft or hard, as essential to producing great results. The key is not simply to achieve results in a micromanaged or authoritative way. It means coaching, mentoring, encouraging, and rewarding leaders and teams to eliminate bullying, fear, and intimidation tactics; to forego manipulations using the carrot-and-stick approach; and to drop demeaning and demoralizing punishment antics that destroy self-esteem. Team members need to know that all such "old-school accountability" methods and behaviors will not be used by management.

On the soft side of change, even the word *discipline* has negative connotations. It conjures up a trip to the school principal's office for a reprimand. *Execution* fares even worse, being associated with punishment or in the worst case, death. *Accountability* also sounds fearful. Therefore, a good leader or manager as coach must *repurpose* these charged words—to show that *discipline* provides individual freedom, support, and empowerment; that *execution* is an agent of offering ongoing feedback, providing innovative solutions that enact change; and that *accountability* means continuous improvement, and learning quickly from both mistakes and best practices, and providing ongoing, positive, peer-to-peer feedback real time. Understood correctly, these are all positive things. The spirit of the *discipline of execution* is based on the feeling that we are all in this together, and that we are here to support, improve, collaborate, and help each other get better over time.

- Colleen Barrett, former vice president of Learning and Development of Southwest Airlines, stated, "Practicing the Golden Rule (always treating people the way you would like to be treated) is integral to everything we do. As it happens, the natural result of applying the 'Golden Rule behavior' is better employee productivity, employee retention, and customer loyalty."[23]

9.
GIVE EFFECTIVE FEEDBACK

All coaches give feedback. Some of it is effective. So what kind of feedback helps you achieve the results you want with your staff? It starts with offering feedback in a balanced way that helps people become better and focusing on their strengths, while helping to target a few key areas for improvement. The spirit of feedback should help to improve, motivate, and build hope—not injure, demoralize, or demotivate. As Albert Schweitzer said, "In everyone's life, at some time, our inner fire goes out. It is then burst into flames by an encounter with another human being. We should all be thankful for those who rekindle the inner spirit."

Usually, we think of feedback as offering the individual our own observations and suggestions. In a coaching context, however, we ask people to give themselves feedback first. Questions to ask people may include these:

- What do you like about what you've done?
- What seems to be working well?
- What would you have done differently?

- What are a few areas you can improve?
- What have you learned? How will you use your new learning?
- What will you do differently in the future?
- What are the benefits of doing things differently?

Only then should you offer, *May I make a few observations and suggestions?*

The people you coach will probably give themselves the feedback you intended to give, and they will take more owner-ship of it if they speak it themselves. Afterward, if necessary, you can always make factual observations and needed suggestions of your own.

During one coaching feedback session with a CEO and his leadership team in their executive conference room, I was present-ing back the summarized data from an employee satisfaction survey that had been given to the entire company. The confidential and anonymous data spoke directly to the issues of goal clarity, goal-execution, translation of goals into action, team synergy, collabora-tion, trust, work-unit relationships, time spent on most-important activities, and commitment to team goals. The data showed big gaps in: poor employee engagement, employee dissatisfaction, people feeling under valued and unappreciated, high absenteeism, and low productivity.

Suddenly, during my report to the senior executive team, the CEO, who also owned the company, shot up out of his chair. Sputtering with anger, he said, "Why should I even care what my employees think? When I was leading crews at this company in the early '60s, people didn't make any crazy statements like this. They didn't have college degrees. They didn't expect all kinds of benefits. They were grateful to have a job, and they kept their mouths shut. Now we have a bunch of entitled whiners and complainers who have way too much time on their hands to sit around and give us feedback."

I had been warned that this CEO's mantras were "If I want your opinion, I'll give it to you," and "Beatings will continue until employee morale improves." Nonetheless, I was shocked by his defensive behavior. Privately, after the meeting, the president, COO, and CFO told me that those types of outbursts and tirades against feedback marked the CEO's management style. The CEO looked me in the eye and said, "Who do you think you are, coming in here and telling me what to do?"

I said, "Sir, with all due respect, this isn't my company data. This is your company data, and you can choose to accept it or not. How you respond or react to your data is your choice. It is simply data. I am here to present you the common themes, trends, and comments that represent all levels of your employee population's perception."

Claiming he had another meeting to attend, he instructed my colleague and me to proceed without him, and he turned and left. (My colleague and I later called this experience "The Scarface Incident" in reference to Al Pacino's portrayal of the famous Mafia leader who led his organization with an iron fist.)

After this, we shifted our focus to coaching the senior team, who were obviously disengaged and resigned to the emotional outbursts of their tyrannical leader. Because the CEO refused to be humble, honest, transparent, and candid—because he insisted on living in the past with its "industrial paradigm" of management—the organization was losing out on tremendous opportunities for honesty, learning, growth, improvement, and renewal.

Although honest feedback provides an excellent avenue to self-awareness and is vitally important to every coaching encounter, it is surprising how often people reject it. The adage "You can lead a horse to water, but you can't make it drink" applies here. Feedback, combined with coaching, can lead to effective and transformational change, but feedback is often squelched or ignored. Employees sometimes fear feedback and don't recognize it's a real, life-sustaining gift to help them improve performance. Ironically, the higher up you go in many organizations, the less likely you'll find managers and senior leaders who embrace or happily receive feedback, so as coaches we have to prepare people to receive honest and helpful feedback.

As we have seen, many organizations continue to deploy a top-down, command-and-control styles of management that allows only limited feedback, with little or no coaching and virtually no peer-to-peer mentoring and support. When fear, victimization, and blame permeate an organization's culture, defensiveness and lack of engagement rules. As Dr. Stephen R. Covey stated, "You can hire someone's hand and back, but you can never hire their heart, mind, and spirit—those must be volunteered."[24] The leader or manager-as-coach can help others see and understand the "whole person" both personally and organizationally. People should be free to bring their hearts, minds, and spirits to work, and will do so when the environment encourages that sort of safety and trust. A dictator thrives on control and fear and perpetuates the old industrial-management approach that is both outdated and ineffective. We are moving from the Industrial Age to the Knowledge Age, when workers expect to be involved and their own intellectual, social/emotional, and spiritual assets are leveraged in the workplace. All too often, people perceive feedback as negative or destructive because the leader communicates that way or avoids giving feedback altogether. Often leaders and managers are not open or prepared to receive feedback themselves, and as a coach you may need to guide them to a new vision of leadership benefits before you can address feedback.

Industrial Age leaders rely on making every decision, telling people what to do and how to do it, and micromanaging their direct reports. Knowledge Age leaders seek to empower people to make their own decisions, being open to feedback, and unleashing the talent of their direct reports towards the organization's goals and priorities. As discussed, the mediocre leader believes they need to constantly control, micromanage, and motivate people with external force. They ride their employees; they never give autonomy to stretch, to expand capabilities, and to grow. These leaders are only interested in short-term, limited results. When change is externally mandated, those under their mandates may comply in the short term but will likely not fully embrace it, and high performance will likely not be sustained. The principle to remember is that when people have no real involvement and ownership over change, they do not have a full commitment to it, and they will resist and resent feedback. The following model reinforces the difference between the industrial age approach and the knowledge age worker approach, with various leadership behaviors and styles that follow. Coaching leaders and managers to use a more participatory style of influence will result in people who are more engaged, trusted, and empowered, and goes a long way to more fully motivate individuals and teams towards sustainable results.

TWO STYLES OF LEADERSHIP INFLUENCE

INDUSTRIAL *(Control)*	KNOWLEDGE *(Release)*
Make every decision	Model high trust leadership behaviors
Boss-centered paradigm	
Tell people what to do	Empower people to make self-directed decisions and manage themselves in
Tell people how to do it	win-win ways
Control system: top-down bureaucracies	Open to feedback and input from employees
Micromanage	Unleash talent towards the highest goals and priorities
External controls; carrot and stick rewards	Create aligned systems, structures, and processes

INDUSTRIAL AGE MANAGEMENT VS. KNOWLEDGE AGE LEADERSHIP

Avoid Negative Reactions

A coach does not need to be the problem solver, psychologist, teacher, advisor, instructor, or even expert. A coach does need to *mirror* the individual, acting as a sounding board, facilitator, and guide to help raise awareness. A great coach believes that people already possess greatness inside themselves; such a person knows that a coach creates a safe zone and the conditions to explore that greatness in the context of personal and professional game plans. Only when people feel safe will they be open to honest feedback and to gaining higher levels of self-awareness based on difficult issues and direct data. As a coach, you can becomes an honest advocate to support and help release the talent and passion towards their individual and organizational goals. An organization or team that creates a culture that actively seeks feedback stands to gain improved leadership and management benefits with faster decision making, quicker course correction, higher performance, employee engagement, and productivity.

Once feedback or assessment is offered, it is common for one-on-one coaching to take place at many levels of the organization. The coach can remind people that feedback is any organization's life-support system and that no organization, team, or individual can effectively improve without it. Both giving and receiving feedback are learned skills, and so, rather than focusing on labeling, fixing, or solving, a coach can be that critical person to objectively help others uncover context, explore themes, and target opportunities for lasting change and performance improvement.

During a three-day leadership work session I was conducting with a bank in Kuala Lumpur, Malaysia, I guided a group through an extensive 360-degree leadership-feedback tool called the Leadership Quotient (LQ). The leaders came to the work session with direct feedback on their leadership capabilities in the areas of: modeling and extending trust; clarifying team purpose and vision; aligning systems, clarifying goals, and unleashing team talent. Many leaders had vast banking experience, whereas others were new but high-potential leaders.

At the end of the second day, I saw one new leader in our session that had reviewed her feedback data and was emotionally upset. She asked for a one-on-one coaching session after the program. I agreed, and during that meeting I asked a series of open-ended coaching questions about how she interpreted the data, what themes she saw, and how she was feeling. The more we spoke, the more visibly upset she became; and she started to cry. She initially expressed shock and rejected the feedback.

After a while, I was able to help her reflect on her new role and think into the future about what she wanted her role and contribution to look like. She began to be more open and explored the data themes honestly from her peers and direct reports. She explored why her team might have given her their responses, and she targeted key insights that could improve her perceptions among her team. She gained new confidence and hope as she narrowed the focus on a few key items and charted a game plan. We identified small, yet significant, steps forward that would help her best leverage her strengths, apply a few key leadership tools, and best influence her team. Initially, there was an absolute shock and sadness based on the data. Over time she moved to humility, self-reflection, and openness and gained a real desire to better understand and work on these newfound insights.

During another coaching session with a senior leader from a large healthcare company, we were reviewing his 360-degree data and discussing his reactions to and his thoughts about general themes, issues, strengths, and areas of improvement from his boss, direct reports, peers, and other key respondents. I had worked closely with this leader for over a year, and had a very high level of trust with him, and I had observed him in many different settings with his team as well as in one-on-one situations. He was a man of great integrity, experience, intellectual capacity, and talent. He consistently delivered results and had the confidence of his executive team. Together we reviewed the three different 360-degree feedback sources from their talent management department, including his annual performance review from his boss. Although he had stellar performance with results, his feedback showed major gaps in his values and behavioral interactions with others. I sought to review his data with him in a balanced way. He could not help but focus and fixate on the negative aspects of the feedback—those areas where he was less than excellent. Coaching feedback offered him a chance to reflect on and reframe his thinking from a solely negative viewpoint to a more balanced view and optimistic approach. Many leaders may react negatively at first and seek to myopically focus on their weaknesses and areas needing improvement, rather than keeping a balanced view. When looking at areas targeted for improvement, it is critical to keep a balance between strengths and weaknesses. Remember to spend time upfront, preparing the performer to have a mindset of continuous improvement. Don't try to do too much. Break down the data, prioritize it, and solicit from the individual the "vital few" areas for which they have energy, interest, and motivation to focus. The key to success is narrowing the focus, keeping it balanced, and not trying to focus on too much change all at once. Improvement areas should focus on targeted stakeholder relationships, specific behaviors, and benefits they expect to receive for acting and behaving in new and better ways.

When using feedback data as a coaching tool, remember that most people tend to look directly at the lower scores and react negatively. Some may automatically go negative and tell themselves a false story, worried that they are failures in every way, even though the data indicate only a few small issues. Avoid trying to solve every issue or gap in the report. Target high and low rankings and frequencies, and the themes or stories that emerge from the quantitative and qualitative data. Avoid ego, avoidance, or resistance by instead giving feedback in ways that help balance and showcase the unique strengths, capabilities, experience, and expertise of the people you are coaching, while also targeting a vital few areas and small steps for improvement. Remember, as Stephen M.R. Covey commonly states, "You cannot talk yourself out of problems you have behaved yourself into, but you can behavior yourself out of those problems rather quickly."

In *Coaching for Performance*, Sir John Whitmore asserts: "Coaching and feedback is about creating a safe environment for awareness and self-awareness to effectively improve. Awareness is knowing what is happening around you. With all people, higher self-awareness is vital for higher performance. Highly effective leaders have high levels of self-awareness, make conscious choices, and self-regulate in proactive ways. They also have high interpersonal understanding. For example, they tend to view themselves and the way others view their capabilities in a relatively consistent manner."[25] Whitmore further notes that some leaders have a highly inflated, overly optimistic view of themselves and their capabilities, whereas others are highly critical of themselves and minimize their capabilities and accomplishments. The key is to find reality, and a coach can raise appropriate levels of interpersonal awareness and self-awareness by using high-quality, relevant data, and asking them how they view their situation and key opportunities based on the data gaps.

How a person responds to feedback determines how willing others will be to give it. It also influences how the other people on the team respond to the feedback they receive. Some feedback can be targeted to provide immediate, short-term benefits; but lasting behavior change, especially as concerns a person's mindset and habits, most often does not happen in a single work session or even after a weeklong workshop. It takes time.

Good coaches give feedback that is a balance of courage and consideration. Courage is willingness and ability to speak honest thoughts and feelings. Consideration is doing so with respect. Great coaches show genuine interest in other people's development, seeing people in terms of their future potential, not just their past performance. Consideration means asking performers how they are interpreting feedback, what relationships or actions they would like to isolate, and what is most important to them about the feedback.

Focus on the Positive

People get energized if they can approach the feedback process openly and positively. As Peter Drucker argues, "Most leaders and employees do not know what their strengths are. When you ask them, they look at you with a blank stare, or they respond to you in terms of subject knowledge—which is the wrong answer." Marcus Buckingham states in his research for improving human performance in his book *Now Discover Your Strengths*, "Leaders must develop a systematic process to help people find out and clarify what their strengths are and how to capitalize on them . . ." Focusing on the positive and playing to people's strengths, as opposed to just focusing on the gaps or closing weaknesses, will go a long way towards empowering, energizing, and motivating people to improve their performance.

Here are some ideas and powerful coaching questions for guiding the feedback process in a positive direction:

- Convey your positive intent. Why are you meeting? What is the purpose of the feedback? Why is it important?
- Describe specifically what you have observed. Identify data, scenarios, evidence, written comments, and events.
- Focus objectively on the data and the behaviors—not the person!
- State the impact of the behavior or action. Focus in a balanced way on the positive strengths and the targeted areas of improvement.
- Ask the person to respond positively. Help the individual see the big picture and frame or reframe the picture in a way that best serves the person's career.

- Leave room for individual initiative. Refrain from telling, directing, or forcing the other person to do things a certain way. Good coaches don't try to fix people; instead, they seek to amplify awareness, choices, and targeted opportunities. You could ask, "What is the data telling you? How did you react to the data? What areas do you feel most motivated to focus on? Do you see any themes or key messages in your data?"

- State your feedback in a way that conveys your sincere courtesy, respect, and support. When you are dealing with a person's deep inner self, you are truly walking on sacred ground. You could ask, "What areas do you see as your greatest strengths? Are there any key relationships that would be important to improve? Do you see any great opportunities for improvement? What would be the benefits of acting on this data? What areas are you most motivated to focus on right now?"

- Respond to what the person receiving your feedback says. You can offer assistance by asking, "How can I be a resource to you? How can the organization or team support you? What other support systems will benefit you?"

- Focus the discussion on solutions and actions. At some point, the data has to be put into simple practice. This means helping the individual to leverage strengths or view things differently. You could ask, "What do you see as being the most important next steps? If you could choose only one or two key items to act on, what would they be? What would you like to act on immediately? In the next 30, 60, or 90 days, what would you like to be different? How will you measure success with your game plan? What would be key milestones or measures for your success going forward? How will you know when you've succeeded?"

It is important for a coach to prepare people for difficult feedback. Some suggestions follow:

- Give people ample time in a private and quiet space to absorb any difficult data.
- Remind them to retain a vision going forward of who they want to be. Remind them to keep a balanced perspective.
- Help them consider gaps, issues, common themes before jumping to hasty generalizations or drastic conclusions.
- Help them see the feedback as a gift—use the proactive muscle of choice and responsibility.
- Help them see how general themes, the rankings and frequencies, the high-end and the low-end scores and comments, can help frame the gaps and opportunities.
- Help them stay away from isolated "left field" or outlier comments.

Qualitative written comments can add tremendous insights to the quantifiable numeric side of the feedback data. Gently guide people to decide what they can learn from their feedback and what seems to be most important for them to focus on or pay attention to. If you're facilitating a group coaching session, give your people a chance to debrief with fellow participants. To help someone feel less isolated, indicate that others have received feedback. Tell stories of how others have used feedback data to launch their lives and careers forward.

When coaching people on their game plan, remember to choose their battles and opportunities wisely. Focus on those targeted areas where you can get quick wins or small victories. Help performers see targeted areas where they can have a positive impact, improve stakeholder relations, or create an opportunity to magnify strengths, overcome weaknesses, and increase personal impact. Agree to a narrowly focused, practical action plan based on data.

When receiving difficult feedback, people may go through certain distinct responses or stages. This is called the SARAH feedback model:

S = Shock. *This feedback doesn't represent me.* Information can create a physical or emotional shock to a person's mind and body, causing great astonishment or disgust. Many times data uncovers blind spots; weaknesses and poor relationships can be exposed at this stage. People may know subconsciously that some of the feedback is true, but now that facts have been brought to a conscious level, they may dismiss them or react negatively or defensively.

A = Anger. The performer might feel attacked, be *mad, closed, withdrawn, annoyed, and/or visibly upset.* The performer may demonstrate extreme displeasure and entertain feelings of personal or team betrayal. "How can they say that about me? Why did they use this tool to be so brutally honest and cruel with their feedback?"

R = Rejection. The performer may attribute negative feedback or problems to other places, circumstances, people, and things. As blind spots get revealed, there can be negative attribution towards people, opinions, and circumstances. It is easy to dismiss, rationalize, or even reject the data.

A = Acceptance. Once the initial sting or shock of the feedback has settled a bit, people may be more open and reflective about looking at the data introspectively and considering why they may feel that way. When the performer feels safe and open to looking honestly at targeted areas of improvement, the performer will acknowledge the data or perceptions as being valid and true. In this stage, the person meets tough issues head on and recognizes that there is validity and accuracy with people's perceptions.

H = Humility/Help. In this stage, feedback is seen as a real gift and opportunity. The performer recognizes the feedback as accurate, motivating this person not only to improve but to seek continuous improvement, to use the data to *proactively* improve, none of which can happen without ongoing feedback. The person is secure and motivated to act on the data for personal benefit and for the team and the organization. They will begin action planning, seek ongoing mentoring and support systems, and truly seek to use the data to get better.

Once people have feedback in a usable form, they need to build a support team to help them stay focused on the implementation. Perhaps those who have gave the feedback can help. Possible team members include:

- The Guide—a person who provides guidance through the change process. This could be the coach's or a mentor's role.
- The Challengers—people who tell the truth, such as a boss, peer, or colleague, or a spouse or partner.
- The Providers—people who provide tangible services or resources, such as a boss or a team member.
- The Comrades—people who are in similar work situations, such as peers or those who may have similar roles or work objectives.
- The Sponsors—people at higher organizational levels, formal or informal mentors, or leaders who provide opportunities for succession planning, career development, expanding roles, jobs, or projects.
- The Diverse—people who help by bringing differing viewpoints, skills, and perspectives. These could be people from different job functions, regions or countries, gender perspectives, or levels within the organization.

10.
TAP INTO TALENT

Much of our history, culture, conditioning, and training grew out of the Industrial Age, where most of the work was routine, and creativity, adaptability, and innovation were not required. It has not been many years since a high percentage of jobs were industrial or traditional in nature.

This culture is rapidly evaporating. Generation-Y and Millennial workers do not want to wait years for job satisfaction: They want it now. They want their talents leveraged, and smart leaders agree with them. Many workers in the millennial era may be better prepared, equipped, and talented in various areas than their boss or job requires or even allows.

Great coaches help to create a culture that unleashes the highest talents and diverse skills and contributions of people. The mindset of a mediocre leader is "My job is to micromanage and control my people to get results." The mindset of a great leader is "My job is to release the talent, passion, and ingenuity of all our people."

Most individuals underestimate their own talents. As a coach you need to know how to help people tap into the unique store of talents and strengths they already have.

Staples founder Thomas Stemberg made it a practice to go from store to store asking workers how he could help them do their jobs better. By doing this simple act, he empowered his employees. In *Winning*, Jack Welch wrote, "Probably the greatest shift you will ever make is the shift of going from a manager to a leader. You will begin to say to yourself, my career success stops being about me and starts being about them."[26]

How can a coach help leaders acquire such an attitude of support, trust, and confidence? It is extremely important that they do because, as Buckingham and Coffman claim in *First Break All the Rules*, how long an "employee stays and how productive he is while he is there is determined by his relationship with his immediate supervisor."[27] If you are an internal coach, you have a tremendous influence over individuals. Every time you open your mouth, you influence the culture of the workplace. You have the opportunity to change and improve employee morale, engagement, and productivity. You can affirm worth and potential by providing encouragement and showing support for your people. You can ignite a fire within people.

To do these things, I recommend that coaches engage in three types of conversations: 1. The performance conversation, 2. The "clear the path" conversation, and 3. The improvement conversation to influence the right focus and behaviors.

Performance Conversation

This conversation, very much like a performance accountability session in the four disciplines process, begins with a win–win attitude. Leaders-as-coaches and team members co-develop and decide together certain desired results and goals. A win–win conversation can happen when conducting annual, mid-year, or quarterly job performance reviews, launching projects, or creating an employee's career development plan. Clear measures of progress are mapped out. What counts as success is clearly defined, and consequences for not succeeding are determined. Those consequences focus on ongoing career, job, educational, or developmental opportunities rather than on punitive measures. This conversation can be held weekly, monthly, or quarterly as needed, and a visible scoreboard is utilized to track success. Here is the agenda I recommend to my clients:

- List the desired results: List desired results, outlining each goal, measure, deadline, and weight of importance by percentage of time spent on each performance objective.
- Guidelines: Set guidelines for key criteria, dos and don'ts, and policies or procedures to be followed.
- Resources: Define the resources needed (people, budgets, technology, facilities, and materials).
- Accountability: Decide on a cadence of accountability—meeting daily, weekly, monthly, or quarterly for performance reviews.
- Consequences: Clarify how the team or individual will benefit from fulfilling the agreement and what the fallout or consequences might be if the agreement is not fulfilled.
- Make sure the Performance Conversation is couched in terms of wins for the organization first rather than just identifying personal wins for individual or team members. Although each contribution is valuable, the overall goal is to achieve the organization's goals and objectives, which, in turn, supports the people who work there.

The following coaching questions can be used for win–win performance conversations. They can be used to create common understanding and clarify expectations during ongoing mid-year and annual performance reviews; to clarify project management goals and objectives among various team members; to align cross-functional groups; and in any situation where clear goals and objectives need to be mutually agreed upon by various customer or stakeholder groups.

WIN-WIN PERFORMANCE AGREEMENT

Agreement Between _____

For _____

Time Period _____

Contribution Statement _____

DESIRED RESULTS

GOAL	MEASURE(S)	DEADLINE	WEIGHT

GUIDELINES
What key criteria, standards, policies, or procedures should be followed?

RESOURCES
What people, budget, and tools are available?

ACCOUNTABILITY
How will we give feedback? How often?

CONSEQUENCES
What are the rewards if the agreement is fulfilled?
What are the consequences if the agreement is not fulfilled?

Improvement Conversation

The Japanese word for continuous improvement is *kaizen*. Coaching requires a focus on *kaizen*, and *kaizen* means being willing to confront weaknesses. Part of the coaching process is to discuss how to improve performance. It must be done in such a way as to increase trust and overcome avoidance and fear. You do this by being respectful as well as honest.

Dr. Stephen R. Covey often talked about how a leader can have high levels of maturity in communication by being both courageous and considerate at the same time. Courage is a willingness and an ability to verbalize thoughts and feelings. Consideration is a willingness and an ability to speak and listen with courtesy and respect. The courageous coach must be honest and direct about goals, measures, targets, laws, rules, regulations, procedures, and issues. At the same time, a considerate coach can give feedback in a way that is kind to people, values, respectful of title, roles, or position, keeping in mind their feelings, capabilities, and valuing differences.

When people feel threatened (for example, if they are criticized, blamed, or given negative feedback), they tend to build up defensive walls to protect themselves. In order to benefit from feedback, individuals might need to work with coaches to reduce defensive behaviors and adopt exploring or open behaviors. Consider the following guidelines when coaching performance improvement:

- Opening statements should be specific, concrete, future oriented, and constructive.
- Comments should be descriptive rather than evaluative. Use objective, factual data and concrete examples rather than subjective impressions or gut feelings.

- Use "I" messages rather than "you" messages. For example, "This is how I am seeing or observing this situation. This is how this situation is showing up for me," instead of "You did such and such."
- Focus on performer's behavior rather than on the person or their personality.

Here are some powerful questions for leaders or managers to help uncover a person's voice, contribution, and potential at an individual and team level:

Individual coaching:

- What specific customer, market, or business needs do you see need to be done on our team? How can you best contribute to satisfy those needs?
- What are you passionate about? What would you be most excited about in your role at work?
- Where are your greatest gifts and talents? What are you really good at?
- What aligns with your values and beliefs?

Team coaching:

- Where could your team add the greatest value within the organization?
- What unique capabilities does your team possess?
- Do you and your people feel valued, appreciated, and recognized for their contribution in their roles?
- What can we do to better recognize and reward top performance with our team?
- How well do you effectively evaluate, develop, and promote the talent on your team?

- How well do you match employees' jobs with the right skills, competencies, and capabilities?
- Does your team have a clear vision, strategy, and goals to drive high performance? How well do you align your talent to drive business strategy and results?
- How well do they execute on their strategic priorities and objectives?

"Clear the Path" Conversation

Once the coach or leader-as-coach has worked together with an individual on building a path to success, it is time to step out of the way—not by abandoning the team, but by stepping aside to let the team do the job for which they have been hired and trained. Micromanagement must become a relic of the past. A study by Harry Chambers in *My Way or the Highway* found that 62 percent of workers have considered changing their jobs due to microman- agement, and 32 percent actually moved out.[28]

The responsibility of a leader or manager-as-coach is to clear the path. Coaching a leader to clear the path can help avoid cultural bureaucracy and barriers by identifying necessary resources and opportunities for people to contribute their best talents. Clearing the path turns traditional supervisors and managers into inspiring leaders who know how to remove obstacles among team members, break down silos, and make work easier for people. There are certain things that are easier for a leader to do than for a team member to do. "Clearing the path" requires leaders or managers-as-coaches to continually ask the team, "What issues or challenge can I help remove? What barriers are getting in the way? How can we help remove obstacles for each other? Who can I talk with to make your job easier?" Identifying and removing roadblocks helps team mem- bers in the trenches realize they are not trying to bring about success alone. Clearing the path also focuses one's efforts on a "stop doing list" of unimportant, non-value added activities such as outdated structures, decision making, policies, practices, meetings, or reports.

Four decades ago, Robert Greenleaf, in his essay *The Servant as Leader*, spoke of a leader's responsibility to clear the path for others: "The servant-leader is a servant first . . . It begins with the natural feeling that one wants to serve . . . Then, conscious choice brings one to aspire to lead . . . The difference manifests itself in the care taken by the servant to make sure their intent is to make sure other people's highest-priority needs are being served first. The best test . . . is this: Do those being served grow as persons? Do they, while being served, become healthier, wiser, freer, more autonomous, and more likely themselves to become servants?"[29]

Success and service beget more success and show others the path ahead with an example to do likewise. As the famous UCLA basketball coach John Wooden said, "There is no leadership if there are no followers. Remember as a coach, you may get full credit for winning, but you didn't win the championships; the players did. They were the ones doing the work."[30]

11.
MOVE THE MIDDLE

Coaches are usually focused on helping high performers get even better. It is essential to recognize and reward top performers, keep them on board, producing, and fully engaged in leading and innovating. However, as previously discussed, the biggest opportunity for performance improvement in any organization is in moving the "middle," among those performers who are good, but not yet great. So how does a good coach take advantage of this opportunity?

During an economic downturn, while many companies were laying off employees, one of my technology clients in Southeast Asia was experiencing massive job growth: from 150 to more than 4,000 workers in a six-year period. It represented great success, but with this almost unbelievable growth came a great challenge: How would the company keep the top talent from leaving the firm, particularly with a shortage of middle- and senior-level talent in Asia and many opportunities calling? The company was hiring about 150 people per month to keep up with both growth and attrition caused by headhunters aggressively luring top talent away.

With another international branch of the same company in India, the situation leaders told me was even more direr. The company had gone from 5,000 to more than 100,000 employees in fewer than eight years! But 70 percent of all new hires had left the company within two years. New hires had come to expect a 30 to 50 percent pay increase just to stay. Thus, the company's challenge in both countries was to keep workers from leaving by the thousands.

Today, there is a lot of legitimate conversation going on about how coaches or coaching can help leaders improve individual satisfaction and job performance. Jack and Suzy Welch talk about "differentiation" in their book *Winning: The Answers*. As they see it, every company has a low-performing group (10 to 20 percent), a middle-performing group (60 to 70 percent), and a high-performing group (10 to 20 percent).[31] Improving team performance in the middle 60 to 70 percent yields the quickest path to greatness. As it turns out, the focus of most coaching is the high-performing group, the top 20 percent. Many firms also get trapped in spending way too much time on the bottom 20 percent trying to convert them to the middle. This is a low value activity since many of these people either won't or can't change. Perhaps focusing our coaching efforts on the 70 percent of the population, the middle performers, would benefit companies more.

TEAM/ORGANIZATIONAL MODEL

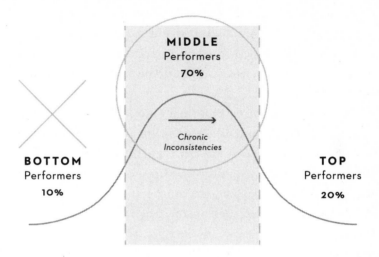

Focus: Reward the top and move the middle

JACK WELCH—GE CORPORATION, DIFFERENTIATION MODEL, BOOK "WINNING"

Source: Jack Welch—GE Corporation. Differentiation Model, from *Winning: The Answers*, Jack Welch with Suzy Welch, New York: HarperBusiness, 2006.

Some simple math makes the point. Imagine that by apply-ing the coaching principles explained in this book, leaders could improve individual performance by 10 percent. If coaching were solely focused on the traditional tier of top performers, a 10 percent improvement in 20 percent of the population would equal 2 percent overall improvement. On the other hand, a 10 percent improvement in the "middle," which constitutes 70 percent of the overall population, would equal a 7 percent improvement overall—more than three times as much! The goal in "moving the middle" is not to ignore top performers, but to spread coaching resources across a larger portion of the performance spectrum. Why not involve both top-level performers and mid-level performers in the coaching initiatives?

The scenario confronting many companies like those in Southeast Asia supports Thomas Friedman's conclusions in his book *The World Is Flat*.[32] He expects a worldwide explosion of job potential for people in the middle, with more opportunities for education and employment. At the same time, the pressure to improve workforce development, promotion, role expansion, and retention will increase. Even when there is a downturn in the economy, there is still a real war for attracting and keeping top talent. A few great leaders cannot fuel growth without sharp, well-trained, and loyal mid-level workers. No company or organization becomes great without moving the middle to higher ground.

Many leaders fail to prepare a talent pipeline for turning mid-level workers into future key management and leadership contributors. When top talent and future leaders leave an organization, money and precious capabilities walk out with them. Virtually every corporation claims its people are its greatest assets, yet the sad irony is that many of those same organizations do not prepare their greatest assets to assume greater leadership roles. Consequently, many mid-level leaders never achieve their potential.

Recently, several members of a company's top management team left their organization. Unfortunately, the senior leader saw the talent departure as a way to improve the organization's bottom line. He imagined that this helped him look good financially as he strengthened his earnings statement and better controlled his earnings before interest and taxes (EBIT) formula. However, those top senior talents took with them skill, experience, mature judgment, and knowledge about revenue growth. They left a void in the company that would be difficult to replace for a long time. The political spin was that the balance sheet would look good over the short term, but the approach threatened the sense of trust in the organization as other members of the team saw through this myopic move and worried about revenue growth and their own positions.

Talent as Asset

Some leaders or managers view top talent as an expense. On the balance sheet, things like facilities, business equipment, and technology investments are usually viewed as assets, whereas people are viewed as an expense. However, in a strengths-based organization, the leader-as-coach should view talent as the greatest asset to acquire, develop and leverage, bar none.

In one of my previous consulting engagements with an aerospace company, they told me that 40 percent of their most senior leaders would retire over the next few years. Obviously, there would be a huge gap in leadership if the new leaders did not emerge from middle management. The company realized that they needed an environment in which untapped talent in the middle could be groomed to ensure succession without risking lowering the middle levels. Here is what they did:

They offered rotating job assignments and coaching for early hires and mid-level managers. No matter the employee's level, they offered one-year job experiences and job rotations on key projects. Targeted employees were mentored to become better leaders as they worked in various team functions and had level-specific job experiences. Their president targeted 65 top talented men and women to be developed as future leaders. They were trained in many ways, including how to reinvent, innovate, manage change, plan, and prioritize projects. These emerging leaders were assigned to run projects, manage programs, and lead functional and cross-functional teams.

Training, coaching, and mentoring leaders and managers required a big investment of time, money, and resources, but all levels within the organization supported the initiative. The executive team viewed coaching as critical because it was transforming individuals, increasing action learning, and leading to better results more quickly. In the midst of difficult economic conditions, with a large percentage of their most experienced talent (Baby Boomers) retiring in the near future, and during a war for top leadership talent, coaching allowed the organization to provide internal support, establish career paths, clarify job assignments, and improve job-rotation experiences for future leaders.

Often, unleashing talent means not only moving the middle performers towards the top but also taking steps to either fix, transition, or eliminate the drag that low performers create on any organization. We all know why the squeaky wheel gets the grease: because it drives us crazy to listen to the loud squeaky wheels. But maybe, instead of constantly greasing the wheel, leaders should respectfully transition, re-assign to new roles, or replace it.

A key aspect of getting the bench strength ready is to move people from functional expertise to broader experiences that provide practical knowledge in the running of projects, managing budgets, building business acumen, and leading people. In academia, a professor cannot teach the theory of music to students for four years, then hand each of them a musical instrument and expect them all to be ready to play in the orchestra. Theory is critical for employees, but expertise means matching theory with practical application. As I reflect upon my own career, I realize that practical work experiences broadened my exposure to a vast world of possibilities and led to my passionate interest in how individuals, teams, and organizations change and improve performance. The leader-as-coach needs to effectively create a talent management system that helps balance conceptual learning with practical, hands-on experience.

An effective leader or coach doesn't simply rely on bringing in new players or looking outside the team every time a shift in strategy occurs. The smartest coaches embed the expectation of change in the organization's work culture and then develop individual talents in existing team members. As Peter Drucker stated, "The greatest role of any leader is to focus on identifying and developing the leadership talents of those around them."[33]

Coach to Create Great Performing Teams

Every organization contains pockets of great performing teams, but interestingly, no discernible difference exists in the basic know-how of the good performers versus the great performers. The key differentiators boil down to two things great performers have been coached to do: execute well and concentrate on reducing inconsistency in bad behavior. A coach can help the middle performers move to higher levels of performance in two ways:

1. The best predictor of future performance is mostly determined by past performance. Identify the existing islands

or pockets of excellence within an organization. To leverage top performance, leaders should find out what the top performers or high-performing teams are doing to produce high-quality results. Leaders must not only capture their strategies but uncover the key competencies, the new and better behaviors, and the attitudes of those who are fully engaged. Using examples and stories of what excellence looks like can inspire and educate others.

2. Ask team members how they can improve their strategic performance, and then provide feedback and support. Establish an environment in which leaders are trained to coach individuals and teams in ways that build upon their strengths and passions. If an individual or a team is stuck, talk about the problems, give appropriate feedback, and address options and opportunities, rather than allow the issues to fly under the radar. The way forward is to name it, reframe it, and provide support to improve it.

Most mid-level workers possess far more capabilities than they are expressing in their current jobs. A good coach thinks of people in terms of their current strengths and future potential, not past performance. A good coach also helps people match their strengths with the right roles. As an executive coach, I have found it helpful to ask employees and leaders all over the world this key talent question: "How many of you possess far more talent, drive, capability, passion, and experience than your current job requires or even allows you to express?" Overwhelmingly, people raise their hands in quiet desperation and say that they are either underutilized, undervalued, or both.

Therefore, coaches must assess how well individuals and teams are developing and improving talents that already exist.

In addition, they need to assess the talent market to bring in the right people from outside the organization. Great leaders and coaches should place much of their highest value work on selecting, developing, positioning, and rewarding high-performing talent.

The competition can copy every advantage a company has except its talent. The world's best talent organizations—like General Electric, Lego, Procter & Gamble, McKinsey, Bain, Berkshire Hathaway, Google, and Microsoft—understand that no matter what size, no matter what type of industry, no matter where they operate globally, their real business is the business of recruiting and building great leaders.

Top-talented people insist on jobs and careers that keep them at the top of their game and give them a path or advantage in their careers. GE's Jeff Immelt says his company has a strong recruiting advantage and attracts top prospects over others because early in their careers, it sends high-potentials to the company's famed Crotonville, New York, leadership-development center. Like GE, great companies provide their own people with the training and opportunities to develop their talents. Great leaders proactively and systematically identify and develop their bench strength. It is critical to cultivate talent at all levels. Leaders-as-coaches must clearly define how they can attract, retain, develop, and reward their employees.

The following coaching questions can help leaders and managers do this:

Attract

- How will you attract the right people that are excited to contribute in their roles and grow within their careers?
- How will you establish the right value-based culture by aligning good HR recruiting processes, rewards and

compensation packages, and career-path opportunities to bring in the right talent?

Position

- Do you have the right players in the right positions?
- Have you clearly identified the right knowledge, skills, and competencies needed for job-specific roles?
- How do you ensure the employees, supervisors, and managers are growing and developing in their roles?
- Have you identified the right competencies and critical skills in order for people to perform their jobs with excellence?
- Do you provide the necessary training, mentoring, and development for people to perform and be successful in their jobs?

Reward

- How do you recognize and/or reward great performance?
- How do you use monetary rewards and non-monetary rewards to drive the right performance and the right behaviors/values?

Coaches can help leaders and managers tremendously by helping them assess their team talent and bench strength. To find out whether you have "the right players on the bus and in the right seats on the bus," answer the following coaching questions:

- List the people on your team.
- Would you hire all of these people again?

- Are these people in the right positions?
- Write the names of those who are stagnating in their roles—who are not being stretched, challenged, developed, or fully utilized.

12.
COACHING: A FINAL WORD

As I work with leaders all around the world, I am amazed by how many attribute their success to someone who believed in them when they didn't believe in themselves.

—Dr. Stephen R. Covey

By now, you should have a better and more confident grasp of how to coach others effectively. We have discussed the foundational paradigms and key principles that are essential to, and foundational for, coaching effectively at any level.

Coaching happens in both formal and informal conversations, short or long, scheduled or unscheduled. Coaching is a focused two-way communication, a meeting of equals challenging assumptions and listening intently to each other. A coaching conversation is not merely a chat, a mere exchange of opinions or advice. It is not where people trade rumors, gossip, play political games, or network. A coaching conversation is one where you intend to listen carefully, understand needs, and fully commit to help people succeed. People should come away from the conversation inspired, empowered, engaged, and equipped with the necessary mindset and tools to be better and do better.

Coaching is a special opportunity. It involves the extension of trust from one person to another at levels and in ways rarely seen in other areas of personal and organizational life. Being someone's coach is both an honor and a responsibility. It balances both individual advocacy and confidentiality with honest and transparent inquiry. Coaches are not there to consult, advise, or tell others what to do, but rather to help them on a road of insight and discovery by using a series of powerful coaching questions. Coaches are entrusted with much. I hope that this book has given you the confidence to lighten the burdens of others and engage and empower them to achieve the greatness that lies within them.

EPILOGUE: COACHING THE ORGANIZATION

Most ailing organizations have developed a functional blindness to their own defects. They are not suffering because they cannot solve their problems but because they cannot see their problems.
—*John Gardner*[34]

To this point, we've talked mostly about coaching individuals or smaller teams. Of course, coaching deals primarily with individuals all the time, but in a sense leaders also have a responsibility to "coach the organization." That means seeing the organization as a whole system.

Millions of people worldwide wake up every day in pain. They suffer with cancer, heart disease, arthritis, or chronic pain in knees, backs, and shoulders. Or they might have an acute condition, such as a traumatic injury or a serious infection. Promoting health and wellness within a complex and interdependent system such as the human body requires understanding of the entire system as a whole. Key health issues can't be addressed at the surface or acute level, but require real diagnosis and then offering various recommendations across the system. We all know pain can stem from a number of causes, including age, illness, inactivity, obesity, injury, or common wear and tear. Doctors may seek to diagnose conditions by doing various tests and then root-cause analysis. Based on their analysis and judgment, they might see the conditions as acute or chronic, which then leads to recommendations, possibly surgeries, and forms of therapy, rehabilitation, medication, follow-up activity, and access to the ongoing services that improve the patient's overall body or system. The goal is to move the patient to full recovery.

On the other hand, doctors also try to promote the overall health and wellness of the patient who is *not* ill. Everyone should have a physical now and then, not only to address any problems but also to pinpoint "opportunity gaps"—things patients can do to improve their wellness, vitality, and quality of life, such as exercise, yoga, meditation, or changes in nutrition.

The same is true for any leader or manager within an organization. All organizations are a series of complex, interdependent systems that consist of a set of subsystems. To coach the organization, leaders must look beyond superficial acute symptoms and cosmetic causes and understand the "root cause-and-effect" relationships of the entire organizational ecosystem. Leaders should also be aware of the opportunities for improving the whole system, from a wellness and a preventative viewpoint, even if it's not "sick."

Quint Studer has said, "Feeling good enough is often the biggest barrier to going to the next level of performance."[35] Jim Collins' way of saying this is: "Good is the enemy of great."[36] "Good enough" is not good enough when the goal is to take the business to the next level. Organizational leaders need to understand the whole system—the pains and the opportunity gaps—in order to change, innovate, and grow, just as they need to understand the whole person in order to coach an individual.

There is a systematic approach to coaching the "whole organization" called the Organizational Effectiveness Cycle (OE Cycle); this diagnostic and design coaching tool can help leaders, managers, and teams get at both acute and chronic issues found in organizations. The OE Cycle is a practical way to understand the dynamic components of the organization and their interrelationships, making it a valuable coaching tool. With the OE Cycle you can easily see and navigate between a lot of complex data to identify gaps in performance and to help provide a common framework and language for people to stand back and understand their own organization.

Presented here is the visual tool and a series of powerful team and organizational coaching questions that help provide clarity and interdependence in the midst of complexity.

ORGANIZATIONAL EFFECTIVENESS CYCLE

Leaders need to be able to see the real problem, not just surface symptoms. The coach's job is to help leaders *see*—to identify and understand the roots of their problems or the strength of their opportunities. The coach empowers them to resolve their own issues, not to depend on others to do it for them. The OE Cycle is a powerful tool for achieving those things.

The OE Cycle has evolved over the years and contains many elements found in: the McKinsey 7S Model, the Burke-Litwin Model, Dr. Covey's Principle-Centered Leadership Model, and had ongoing input from David Hanna's breakthrough work in organizational behavior found in The Performance Capability Cycle. Many consultants and coaches have used it in thousands of engagements to help leaders "get their arms around" the entire organization with its interplay of parts, and understand where to target and prioritize their efforts to improve the whole system.

The value of the OE Cycle is that it gives leaders and managers an overall picture of the health of their organization. The OE Cycle enables a coach to achieve these purposes:

- Analyze and agree on the root causes of best and worst results.
- Identify current performance gaps and share a vision of better results.
- Identify high-leverage organizational misalignments that prevent better results.
- Correct misalignments and create new cultural behaviors.
- Share a "holistic" action plan for change.
- Measure and evaluate the impact of the implemented changes.
- To help organizations stay focused on satisfying the needs and the results required by key customers, stakeholders, and the marketplace.

The old saying by Arthur Miller is still true: "All organizations are perfectly designed to get the results they get." If an organization desires to change, it should start by analyzing the paradigms and choices that are getting its current results. The OE Cycle brings us around to that understanding. Business results are the product of the operating principles, paradigms, and assumptions you have about serving your customers, your vision and mission, your core systems and processes, your cultural value and behaviors, and your people. Your effectiveness as an organization depends on the mindset and operating principle you have about aligning each of these things. That's why the purpose of the OE Cycle is first of all to challenge your assumptions about:

- your key customers, stakeholders, market, and community needs;
- your vision and mission;
- your strategy, strategic narrative, and goal execution system;
- your core processes, structures, and systems; and
- your values, culture, and talent management

Your assumptions about each of these topics drive your most important business results, both external and internal.

How do you use the OE Cycle as a coaching tool for an organization? The same way you coach an individual: by asking powerful coaching questions. In fact, you could describe the OE Cycle as a series of questions that, if taken in sequence, lead to a deep understanding of the reasons you're getting the results you're getting. Remember, we are all perfectly designed and aligned to get the results we get—at the individual, team, and organizational level.

We're going to drill down into each segment of the OE Cycle. Mostly what you will encounter are powerful coaching questions that help leaders discover and grasp the issues they need to focus on to improve the organization.

Customer/Stakeholder/Market Needs

At this stage, the coach works with leaders to define customers and stakeholders, focusing on why the team and the organization exists and whom they are ultimately in business to serve in the marketplace or community. The coach asks:

- Who are your customers, both internal and external? What other stakeholders are key to your success—your employees, colleagues, industry associations, community groups or members, and/or social media?
- Select your top four or five customers and/or stakeholders that are critical to your organization's success. How well are you currently satisfying those top customers and stakeholders?
- What do you need to do to better satisfy their needs?
- What unique value do you provide to the markets and the communities you serve?
- What is your competitive advantage? How do you differentiate yourself based on the value you provide to those you serve?

Don't take this discussion lightly. Feel free to discuss some or all of the following strengths, weaknesses, opportunities, and threats with your current state results, in the context of your desired future state results, that may include: customer satisfaction and loyalty, market share, market growth, market position, market leadership, stock price, shareholder return, investment, strategic partnerships or acquisitions, brand image, valuation, profit, cash flow, debt reduction, liquidity, operating costs, operating quality, speed to market, working capital, employee satisfaction and loyalty, work climate and culture, values, talent management, performance management, and training and development.

At the team level, leaders or coaches must help members focus on executing strategic goals that satisfy specific customer and stakeholder needs. For example, team leaders and team members must know how they individually drive such things as cash, sales growth, margin, profit, managing debt, and many other issues, including reward and recognition, and work–life balance. With this information, the team can move forward towards "true north," being better aligned with the vision, mission, and values of the overall organization.

Vision, Mission, and Values

At this stage, we examine our vision (our view of ourselves into a desired future state), our mission (our reason for existing), and our values (our code of conduct in the marketplace).

We call this stage "Identifying True North"—in which direction are we heading? As a coach, your task is to use directed questions to help leaders map out a course instead of "wandering around" aimlessly without direction as an organization. Here are some general questions that can help define true north for your organization or team.

- Do you have a clear vision and mission?
- Why do you exist as a company/team? Who do you serve?
- What unique value do you provide to those you serve?

- How do you see yourself as an organization in a year? Five years? Ten years?
- What are the key principles and values that guide how you act and behave as an organization?
- How do you reconnect and recommit your people to your vision, mission, and values in an ongoing way?

Vision

Vision differs from mission in that the organization is trying to see itself "down the road." It's about where you will be and what success will look like as an organization in the future. To get at vision, coaches can ask:

- What do you truly want to become in a year? Five years? Ten years?
- What is your potential as an organization?
- What will success look like when you have achieved your future state?
- Is this vision one that is shared with others? Will it inspire them?
- What kind of inspired effort are you prepared to put in to achieve such a vision?
- What measures need to be in place so you can tell whether you're achieving your vision?

An organizational vision statement is made up of two elements: a compelling description of a future state and a "stretch goal."

The compelling description describes what you aspire to become, to achieve, or to create as an organization. It's a dream of the future, a mental image of the end in mind—a vivid description, if possible. For example:

In five years we will be the largest pharmaceutical delivery service in the country. People everywhere will be getting life-saving and pain-reducing prescriptions through us on time and in perfect order. No one will be better than we are. In ten years, we will be the market leader by having 65 percent market share.

A stretch goal is a big challenge that elicits the best people can give. It provides a "gulp factor" when it dawns on people what it will take and the level of commitment actually required to achieve the vision. For example:

In ten years, we will have the best on-time delivery record in the business, which means we must go from a 77 percent to a 95 percent rate of on-time delivery. And that's a stretch.

Mission

Your mission says what you are about, your purpose and fundamental reason for being. A great mission inspires people and mobilizes their energy, tapping their idealism rather than just creating an "output." Deeper questions you can ask to get at mission:

- What is or could be the unique contribution this organization makes—a contribution nobody else can make?
- Who are you really? What is the nature of your relationship to the marketplace or those you serve?
- Who are the key markets and customers you choose to serve?
- What are you the best at? What are you not best at?

- Is your mission truly inspiring, challenging, or motivating?
- Can you really live by the mission you have in mind for yourselves?

Senior leaders must lead the development of the mission, but others will not own it unless they are socialized and involved significantly, intensely, and *early*. There should be widespread review and feedback, with particular concern for integrating sub-unit missions or onboarding new people to the mission and purposes of the organization.

Even if the organization is already satisfied with the mission, here are some diagnostic questions that should be asked:

- Are you living up to your mission? How do you know?
- Does your mission pertain to everyone in the organization? Are some ignoring it or acting outside of it?
- Does everyone know the mission? Do all believe in it, live by it, and model it?
- Does the mission reflect who we are and who we serve?
- What symbols or examples do we have of people actually living our mission?
- Does the mission need adjusting or amending in any way?

Values

Values should be explicitly expressed in both the mission and the culture. Values are the organization's internal code of conduct. They apply to everyone personally and professionally. "People in business talk a lot about mission and values," says Jack Welch. "But too often the result is more hot air than real action. No one wants it that way, but the loftiness and the imprecision inherent in both terms always seem to make it end up like that."[37]

The coach's task is to help make sure that the organization's values are *precise* and not too lofty. Everyone is in favor of honesty and integrity, of course, but what are the exacting values and behaviors that your organization should live by? Coaches can ask:

- What values do you need to live by to ensure that you fulfill your vision and mission?
- If you were to start a new company tomorrow, what values would you build into your organization?
- What values excite you? What values are distinctive to your organization and its culture?
- Can you envision yourself living by those organizational values?
- How will you know whether you are living by these values? What measures and processes will you put in place to assess whether people are living up to your values?
- How will you avoid cynicism about your values? How will you socialize or institutionalize your core values?
- What consequences are you willing to live with if people do not live up to or seek to model your organizational values?

Most great organizations are distinguished by a strong vision, mission, and values.

For example:
The Walt Disney Company
Vision: Ultimately, our goal is to be the most admired company in the world.

Mission: Disney's mission is to always deliver, with integrity, the most exceptional entertainment experience for people of all ages.

Values: We believe we can achieve this goal by conducting our business and creating in an ethical manner, and by promoting the happiness and well-being of kids and families by inspiring them to join us in creating a brighter tomorrow.[38]

Strategy

The strategy is the path or plan. The goal of strategy is to leverage and focus all of a company's key organizational resources to add significant value and competitive advantage in order to win in the marketplace with those customers they choose to serve. At this stage, the coach's job is to challenge assumptions about organizational strategy:

- What strategy would completely fulfill the mission, vision, and values of the organization?
- How does your current strategy advance your mission? Your vision? Your values?
- How do you differentiate yourself from your competitors? In what ways do your customers see you as distinctive? Why do they buy from you and how can you sustain a competitive advantage with the products and services you offer?
- What is your strongest competitive advantage?
- What is exciting about this strategy? Are people motivated by it? Inspired?
- What is your current business situation? How will your strategy help close the gap between your current state and your vision of where you want to be?
- What core resources do you need to have in order to compete and close that gap?

The Strategic Narrative

The Strategic Narrative helps leaders, managers, and teams develop and communicate the complexities and aspects of their overall strategy into a clear, practical, and focused "one-page storyline" to achieve the future strategy and goals over a two- to five-year period.

- What is your strategic context? What are the key external forces impacting your business to change?
- What is your job to be done as defined by your customers and stakeholder needs?
- What is your money-making model (for profit)? Or, what is your resource generation model (non-profit)?
- What are your core capabilities?
- What are your strategic bets or strategic goals and objectives that will help you deliver your vision over the next two to five years (list key targets and measures)?
- Do you have a clear one-page strategic narrative that you can clearly communicate to your business unit or team that showcases your vision, purpose, strategies, and goals to win and compete in the marketplace over the next two to five years?
- How will you know the strategy is working?
- Is your strategic narrative concise, easy to understand, compelling, motivating, and realistic?

Strategic Goals (WIGS)

At this stage, the task of the coach is to help leaders translate the strategy into a limited set of "Wildly Important Goals"—a set of no more than one to three of your most important strategic goals that must be achieved this year or nothing else really matters much. You can help the team focus and arrive at these goals by asking these questions:

- What must you do and what are the measurable outcomes to make your strategy successful?
- What goals are primary—absolutely must-haves—as opposed to secondary goals—nice to have?
- Can you get your primary wildly important goals down to a manageable number? No more than one to three?
- How will you measure success on each goal? What is your "X" (current state)? What is your "Y" (desired state)? By when must you close the gap between X and Y?
- What exactly will you and others do to achieve the goal? What actions are in your control? What can you influence at least 80 percent of the time?
- Are scoreboards clear and easily accessible to everyone involved in reaching the goals?
- Can you measure and see if you are winning or losing on the goals?
- How often will you meet to assess progress and accountability on the goals?
- Are your team goals aligned to achieve organizational goals?
- Do you have the necessary resources to accomplish your goals?

Without clear, measurable goals, a tracking system, and frequent, regular accountability, a team has little chance of fulfilling the strategy. It's the job of the leaders to make sure these things are in place.

Systems, Structures, and Processes (The Six Rights)
Every team has a core work process or system. Some teams sell, some create products, some regulate or audit, some pay bills, some

directly serve customers, and so forth. The coach's task is to challenge leaders on whether the systems, structure, and core processes actually support the strategy.

Often, core processes and bureaucratic structures may stem from an old paradigm and need reworking to align with a new strategy. The core processes can make things more efficient and improve quality of service, or they can suppress energy and creativity. All processes must first begin with the needs of the customer or stakeholder, and then be linked to the strategy. The coach should ask:

- What is your core work process? Can you accurately describe the workflow? Can team members describe it?
- Is there physical evidence of the process, for example, a document that describes it in step by step detail?
- Who is served by the process? Are these people happy with the service they are getting?
- Does the current process adequately support the organization's mission, vision, values, and strategy? Why or why not?
- Is there an ongoing feedback loop so that you can tell whether the process is working well?
- Does the process align with other processes in the organization?
- Do you have a process for continually improving the core process?
- Is the core process independent of the leader? Will it outlast the leader?

Talent, Culture, and High-Trust Behaviors

You have a mission, vision, values, strategy, goals, and core processes to achieve the goals. It's time to assess your "talent system," that is, the way you recruit, develop, and promote your talent, build a culture, and reward your people. Your people are by far your most important asset, and the coach's task is to ensure that the organization is getting the best people and leveraging their talents and modeling the right values while in service of the mission and the customers. Ask these questions:

Talent

- How do you attract and select the best people to work on your team?
- What can you do to become more attractive to recruit and retain top talent?
- Do you have the right people in the right positions? How do you know?
- Does your team have the key capabilities to drive the strategy? If not, how will you fill that need?
- Who are your key people? What are you doing to develop them into the next generation of leaders?
- Do you have a system for discovering and leveraging the talents of your people?
- Does each of your key people have a clear development plan?
- Do you have the right internal or external training opportunities available for people to improve their capabilities? Why or why not?

Culture

Culture is defined as the common attitudes and behavior characteristic that are displayed by the majority of a group or organization, the majority of the time. Developing a culture where employees feel valued, respected, and recognized as important and trusted individuals helps move away from the industrial model with its micromanagement approach to one of a self-directed, high-performance company. Great leaders know how to build the right culture of performance by providing the right rewards and recognition, so they do it consistently. The following coaching questions will help leaders build an aligned culture:

- How do you recognize and reward your best talent and great performance?
- Is your compensation system aligned with the mission, vision, values, and strategy? Are people actually rewarded for doing the right things?
- How simple and transparent is your "total reward program"?
- Do your people at all levels feel they are paid equitably based on fair market, industry, and individual contribution measures?
- Would people generally feel that rewards and recognition programs are based on fair, rational, and objective criteria as measured by high performance results and adherence to great values?

What a difference it makes to have what are the most important goals of the organization translated down to what is most important to the individual. There should be no guessing about where the organization is going and how success will be measured, even at the individual level.

Results

Of course, the point of the OE Cycle is to help leaders diagnose and access their organizational system, processes, and culture in order to design and align teams and the organization to get better results. The coach's task is to make sure leaders track the results of the Cycle and continually revisit the Cycle. To a great extent, a leader's work is to think always in terms of the Cycle and never stop asking the challenging questions that make up the Cycle. As a coach, you can start this process by asking:

- What do you predict will be the key intended results based on your design work with the Organizational Effectiveness Cycle?
- What are your most important external results?
- What are your most important internal results?
- How will you know whether you are actually meeting key customer and stakeholder needs?
- What measures do you or will you have in place to determine whether you are truly fulfilling your vision and mission?
- Has your organization clearly defined its core values, behaviors, competencies, and culture?
- How will you be able to tell whether the organization is living up to its values?
- How will you be able to measure the effectiveness of your culture? What mechanism do you have in place for measuring and improving them?

The OE Cycle is an ideal coaching tool for helping organizations align their executive team focus on closing the right gaps and opportunities for continuous improvement.

While coaching at a large global accounting firm, I had introduced the OE Cycle as a coaching tool to their partners and directors to help build a common language to diagnose, design, and work through some very difficult organizational changes. As they applied this framework, this tool helped them target on and focus some very important issues:

- They established a burning platform for change. They understood that people must see and understand the "strategic why" and the business case for change. People must understand the key gap areas and the benefits of change.

- They developed a clear and compelling vision of their desired future state and the rationale for communicating their change effort. They articulated how this change effort would positively impact their markets, customers, and stakeholders.
- They linked strategy with the money making model, and how they would leverage their core resources and clarify their overall goals.
- They identified aspects of their new culture and climate. They identified some key gap areas to better model and live their espoused values.
- They put a detailed change communication plan in place. They realized if they didn't proactively influence the message at all organizational levels effectively, they knew that somebody else would control the messaging, and it likely would not be positive.
- They created two-way communication and dialogue processes to allow constructive and honest feedback and input during change. They knew that in the midst of major changes as an organization, nobody has all the right answers.
- They took time to coach and help clarify how the change would benefit others. They also gave time for people to buy in, assimilate, and recalibrate in their new roles.
- They accepted that change is a process and that transformation would not happen overnight. It was a marathon, not a sprint.
- They were persistent. They stayed on message; they stayed involved with people and on course during the

process of adoption, ownership, and implementation of change.

- They alleviated fears and concerns in an honest and transparent way. They knew trust and good intent were the key. They helped people remain proactive and stay in their areas of direct influence.

Some change efforts can be superficial, short-term focused, myopic, or not well planned at all. Organizational change efforts are never easy. However, if done right, the rewards are immense. Although critical, the rewards of change are more important than getting financial cash and profit margin. Coaching is one of the most powerful tools to getting engagement, involvement, and motivation—the best out of every employee. Coaching involves making sure each person in the organization knows their part of the change effort and has a key role and is empowered to play in that transformational effort. Coaches can help teams and organizations view change as an opportunity to learn, adapt, reinvent, get better, and align all of the organizational resources and structural changes to advance the new vision forward. The OE Cycle offers a comprehensive lens and tool to better "see and understand" the various elements and dynamics of change, including: key stakeholders' satisfaction and results, the vision, the strategies, and the goals to be achieved. It also helps to see the critical need for the right paradigms, principles, people, and culture necessary to positively affect change as well. Coaches can help leaders and teams ask the right questions, such as: the why and the purpose for change, who needs to be involved, who will sponsor, and the step by step processes needed to navigate successfully. Coaches can help leaders plan and implement these important decisions. Coaches can be a guide on the side, or in some cases, right in the trenches to move people and organizations towards greatness. The ultimate outcome of coaching during organizational change is to achieve key business results, while at the same time to help employees become more focused, productive, engaged, satisfied, and happier at work.

NOTES

1 www.gallup.com/consulting/52/employee-engagement.aspx. Gallup—Harter, Schmidt, Killham, and Agrawall, Q12 Meta-Analysis, August 2009 http://www.handsupincentives.com/wp-content/uploads/2011/10/Employeeengagement_Q12_WhitePaper_2009.pdf
2 Columbia University Business School Research 2008
3 A complete list of the ICF Ethics & Regulations can be found at http://www.coachfederation.org/about/ethics.aspx?ItemNumber=850&navItemNumber=621
4 *The SPEED of Trust: The One Thing That Changes Everything* Stephen M. R. Covey, 2008, 384 pp (New York, Free Press, 2006)
5 *The Last Lecture* by Randy Pausch (Hyperion, 2008)
6 *The Feeling Good Handbook, The New Mood Therapy* by David D. Burns (Plume; Revised edition May 1999)
7 *Change Your Questions, Change Your Life* by Marilee Adams (Berrett-Koehler Publishers, June 2009)
8 Some of these coaching questions are drawn from the GROW Model, developed by Sir Jonathan Whitmore, and are exclusive

property of Corporate Learning Solutions Group, Columbia University.

9   *The 7 Habits of Highly Effective People* by Stephen R. Covey (Simon & Schuster Ltd; Revised edition January 1999)

10 *Flow: The Psychology of Optimal Experience* by Mihaly Csikszentmihalyi (HarperCollins, October 2009)

11 *Flow: The Psychology of Optimal Experience* by Mihaly Csikszentmihalyi (HarperCollins, October 2009)

12 Amy Shipley, "Dara Torres Pursues Speed for the Ages," *Washington Post*, May 16, 2012, http://articles.washingtonpost.com/2012-05-16/sports/35456682_1_dara-torres-bruno-darzi-middle-aged-woman

13 Watson Wyatt Survey, "Work USA 2004/2005"

14 KPMG 2000 Global Organizational Integrity Study https://www.kpmg.com/US/en/IssuesAndInsights/ArticlesPublications/Documents/kpmg-integrity-survey-2013.pdf

15 *The Speed of Trust* by Stephen M.R. Covey (New York, Free Press, 2006)

16 *The Heart Aroused: Poetry and the Preservations of the Soul of Corporate America* by David Whyte (Crown Business; Reissue edition, December 2007)

17 The History Place, Great Speech Collections, Speech given by President John F. Kennedy, September 12, 1962, http://www.historyplace.com/speeches/jfk-space.htm

18 Harvard Business School's Michael Porter, *Six Disciplines Execution Revolution* by Gary (Harpst, 2008 page 30, quoting Michael Porter)

19 *Execution Essentials* by Stephen R. Covey (RosettaBooks January 2014)

20 Harris Interactive Survey commissioned by FranklinCovey *The 8th Habit: From Effectiveness to Greatness* by Stephen R. Covey 370 pp.; add space after (Free Press, New York, 2004)

21 *CEO Challenge 2011: Fueling Business Growth with Innovation and Talent Development* by Charles Mitchell (April 2011). http://www.conference-board.org/publications/publicationdetail.cfm?publicationid=1921

22 Quote from Kurt Lewin's research on Force-field Theory (1890-1947); he was a social psychologist whose extensive work covered studies of leadership styles and their effects, work on group decision-making, the development of force field theory, the unfreeze/change/refreeze change management model, action research, and the group dynamics approach to training, especially in the form of T-Groups. Lewin founded the Center for Group Dynamics at the Massachusetts Institute of Technology (now based at the University of Michigan).

23 *Character First The Magazine,* Colleen Barrett on Leadership at Southwest Airlines, Krista Born, November 29, 2011. http://www.cfthemagazine.com/2011-12/colleen-barrett-on-leadership-at-southwest-airlines

24 *The 7 Habits of Highly Effective People: Powerful Lessons in Personal Change* by Stephen R. Covey (Simon & Schuster Ltd; Revised edition January 1999)

25 *Coaching for Performance* by Sir John Whitmore (Nicholas Brealey Publishing; Fourth edition, October 2009)

26 *Winning* by Jack Welch with Suzy Welch (HarperBusiness; 1st edition April 2005)

27 *First Break All The Rules* by Marcus Buckingham and Curt Coffman (Simon & Schuster; First edition May 1999)

28 *My Way or the Highway: The Micromanagement Survival Guide* by Harry Chambers (Berrett-Koehler Publishers November 2004)

29 *The Servant as Leader Essay* by Robert Greenleaf (The Greenleaf Center for Servant Leadership, January 2008)

30 *Quotable Wooden: Words of Wisdom, Preparation, and Success by and about John Wooden, College Basketball's Greatest Coach* by John Reger (Taylor Trade Publishing; Updated edition January 2012)

31 *Winning: The Answers* by Jack Welch with Suzy Welch (HarperCollins October 2006)

32 *The World Is Flat* by Thomas Friedman (Farrar, Straus and Giroux; 3rd edition August 2007)

33 *The Effective Executive: The Definitive Guide to Getting the Right Things Done* by Peter F. Drucker (HarperCollins e-books; Revised edition October 2009)

34 *7 Early Warning Signals of Decline* by Donald B. Bibeault, page 61, Corporate Turnaround: How Managers Turn Losers Into Winners!

35 *Understanding Workplace Cultures & Forms*, by Quint Studer, February 22, 2012, page 34

36 *Good to Great* by Jim Collins (HarperBusiness; October 2001)

37 *Winning* by Jack Welch with Suzy Welch (HarperBusiness; 1st edition April 2005) page 22

38 Disney Citizenship Performance Summary 2012, The Walt Disney Company, page 9.

ACKNOWLEDGMENTS

Unlocking Potential would not have been possible without the support from many amazing people. Thanks to all those who have unlocked my potential and to those who continue to unlock the talent and passion of those around them.

My beautiful wife Cynthia and our four boys: Zachary, Luke, Jacob, and McKay. I am appreciative of their ongoing encouragement, love, and support.

With deep gratitude and thanks to my parents, Steven and Veronica Brand, and to my siblings Sabrina and Brent. To my late father, Kenneth G. Simpson, and to the positive influences of my extended family: George and Louise Simpson, Hugh and Beth Brand, David and Vickie Reeves, David and Kristi Reeves, Mark and Debbi Reeves, Jeff and Lisa Reeves, Cam and Steffani Packer; each models the importance of family, faith, and commitment.

To my clients. I learn more about leadership and coaching from you than I could ever imagine.

To Columbia University's Executive Coaching Certification Program, and my colleague, Dr. Terry Maltbia, who is truly a master teacher and coach to so many. He has been the single biggest influence in my life in my role as a coach.

My colleague and friend Fatima Doman whose professional insights to coaching have been invaluable; her dedication to coaching is inspiring. To Sam Bracken's brilliance, persistence, and support with this project was monumental.

To those who offered editorial guidance and input during the difficult task of writing this book. Many offered unique insights, writing, editing, formatting, and contributions, including: Dr. Breck England, Dr. Dean Collinwood, Dr. Terry Maltbia, Annie Oswald, Zachary Kristensen, Echo Garrett, Richard Godfrey, Terra Davis, and Steffani Packer.

To FranklinCovey's corporate executive team. I am motivated by your pursuit of leadership excellence around our vision and mission to: "Enable greatness within people and organizations everywhere!" including: Bob Whitman, Sean Covey, Shawn Moon, Todd Davis, Scott Miller, Steve Young, and Colleen Dom. A special thanks to Tammy Faxel and Dan Byrne, for having a vision for this book, providing honest feedback, suggestions, and editing improvement throughout the process of book design, development, distribution, marketing, and promotion.

To FranklinCovey's international partners. Thanks for allowing me the opportunities to innovate, teach, and facilitate many of these coaching models and tools with your diverse and passionate clients. To our senior consultants and coaches, general managers, and practice leaders. Your desire to modeling principle-centered leadership with clients and within your regional teams helps to *Unlock Potential* and positively influence the lives of so many people. To our client partners and colleagues. Your hard work and dedication to customer loyalty as trusted partners with both clients and consultants is unprecedented.

ABOUT THE AUTHOR

Michael K. Simpson has been one of the world's preeminent leadership and executive coaching experts to many of the top businesses in the world for more than twenty-five years. As an author, speaker, coach, and senior consultant at FranklinCovey—he was on faculty for three years teaching at their Executive Leadership Summit with Dr. Stephen Covey, Dr. Ram Charan, and Dr. Mette Norgaard. Some of Michael's clients include: Marriott, GE Capital, Frito-Lay, Lilly, Nike, John Deere, ExxonMobil, Hewlett Packard, HSBC Bank, Highmark, Prudential, ING, TE Connectivity, and Coca-Cola, to name a few.

Formerly, Michael was a Principal Consultant for the global management consulting firm PricewaterhouseCoopers (PwC) in their Strategic and Organizational Change practice in New York City, NY. He also held executive management positions for two leading technology companies as Vice President of Sales and Marketing and Vice President of Business Development.

In addition to his practical, real world business experience, Michael brings academic acumen to his work, having been an adjunct professor in the School of Business at Columbia College and a professor at the South China University of Technology in Guangzhou, China. His co-authored and published works include: *Ready, Aim, Excel* with Dr. Marshall Goldsmith and Dr. Ken Blanchard; *Your Seeds of Greatness,* leadership quote books with Dr. David Paxman; *Talent Unleashed*; *The Execution-Focused Leader* with PricewaterhouseCoopers; and *Building Organizational Trust,* co-authored with Stephen M.R. Covey.

Michael has a master's degree in Organizational Behavior from Columbia University, and a bachelor's degree in International Relations from Brigham Young University.

When he's not busy traveling and coaching executives worldwide to optimize their team performance, Michael enjoys traveling, skiing, tennis, and spending time with his family in the beautiful Wasatch Mountains of Utah.

Contact Michael K. Simpson at www. simpsonexecutivecoaching.com

For more information on this and other FranklinCovey products and services, go to www.franklincovey.com